Praise for Sherris and Her Book

"This book feels like a blueprint for the peace of mind I crave. I love the way Sherris interweaves the essence of what it means to heal and thrive into the profound truths that unlock self-discovery and deep, healing connection. I feel like my mind and heart—my whole person—can embrace my innate power even more because of the wisdom inside this book. Thank you, Sherris."
—*Lori Hammond, professional hypnotist and teacher, Colorado, USA*

"Without Sherris and the therapeutic hypnosis session, the impact of our event would have been less profound. Sherris truly enhanced the quality of our conference. I am passionate about therapeutic hypnosis and wanted to share its transformative power in a live session with our event participants. On the morning of day two, Sherris led a subconscious library process that allowed our participants to effortlessly address and release something that may have been difficult for them. This experience opened their minds, hearts, and souls to a deeper and more intimate understanding of our work together. Sherris adeptly addressed curiosity and change, bypassed conscious resistance, and guided our participants to experience change in a new way."
—*Madeleine MacRae, CEO of Legacy Leadership Institute, Florida, USA*

"Sherris, you have completely transformed my life, and I am so grateful!"
—*Paul Baldwin, Washington DC, USA*

"Absolutely life-changing experience! My sessions with Sherris have been incredibly transformative. Her expertise, professionalism, and genuine care have helped me overcome challenges I never thought possible. I am truly grateful for the positive impact she's had on my life. I highly recommend her to anyone seeking real and lasting change!"

—*Sevil Onan Rochester Hills, Michigan, USA*

"Sherris is awesome. She takes the time to understand your situation and come up with a plan to best help your needs. As someone who likes to learn, I really appreciate her explaining the process and helping me understand what we are working on."

—*Nick Theisen, Birmingham, Michigan, USA*

"There aren't words to truly express how much Sherris saved me. I was in such a low place in my life after a sudden breakup and feeling lost in the rest of my life. After my sessions, within a few days, I felt like a new person (my old happy self)—a woman I hadn't seen for so long. My family and friends couldn't believe the difference either. I feel peace, joy, hope, strength, and happiness again! I will be forever grateful for Sherris and her compassion and skills as a hypnotherapist. Best money I have ever spent!"

—*Sara Sloan, Milford, Michigan, USA*

"I hired Sherris for several hypnotherapy sessions. She has been great to work with and has a way of making you feel calm, comfortable, and free to share. I'm very happy with the progress I have made, and I believe it would not have been possible without her assisting me. She also takes the time to explain how hypnotherapy works and what to expect. I'd highly recommend Sherris if you are interested in hypnotherapy. She's amazing!"

—*Julie Spengler, Florida, USA*

"Through her unique style of hypnotherapy, Sherris guided me to those difficult places that required healing in order to propel me to the truest version of myself. Today, for the first time, I feel happy and complete with all aspects of myself. Sherris is a gifted healer and spirit guide who I highly recommend."

—*Lila Pappal, Bloomfield Hills, Michigan, USA*

"I first came to Sherris because I was dealing with anxiety and low confidence in my work and personal business. By the first session, she had gotten to the root of my issue, and everything made so much sense. I have been to other therapists all my life, and none of them have ever spoken and got through to me like Sherris. After a few months, my anxiety has diminished, and my boundaries with people are so much stronger. You just feel different in the best possible way. I will continue to keep coming to Sherris and recommend everyone dealing with something to talk to her."

—*Katherine Green, Farmington, Michigan, USA*

"My hypnotherapy sessions went great! I booked my session with Birmingham Clinical Hypnotherapy because I felt stuck subconsciously. It's been about three weeks, and I no longer feel stuck. There has been an overflow of abundance of love, money, and appreciation coming to me ever since! Thank you, Sherris."

—*Javar Fields, Florida, USA*

"My experience with Sherris was life-changing. She helped me find my parental voice and see myself as a source of love, strength, light, and more. I am so grateful for Sherris's gentle voice and effective guidance, and I was amazed that the handful of sessions with her were more effective than the dozens of sessions I'd had with my traditional therapist. Thank you, Sherris!"

—*Cheri Baker, Birmingham, Michigan, USA*

"The work I did with Sherris is life-changing! She has helped me go deep within myself to uncover the root causes of my anxiety and self-doubt and has given me the tools to overcome them. After three sessions, I feel empowered to continue the work on my own with the help of the recordings Sherris supplied me with."

—*Brendan O'Leary, Royal Oak, Michigan, USA*

"Sherris changed my life. I was in a negative mindset that even therapy could not adequately address. This warm, intelligent, perceptive, and honest woman taught me about the power I had within my own mind to be happy again. The tools and new habits I gained through hypnotherapy turned everything around! I love life, and I love and trust myself again. Unbelievably incredible experience!"

—*Gayle Bowman, Detroit, Michigan, USA*

"I highly recommend working with Sherris. Everything from the environment to the personalized experience she creates makes for an incredible experience of self-discovery. I'm very grateful for the work we did!"

—*Ryan Lax, Birmingham, Michigan, USA*

"My son had a bad case of vertigo. Once he started to recover, he developed a case of social anxiety. He would not leave the house. A colleague from work recommended Sherris to me. She had a great deal of success with his son, who had similar anxiety challenges. We signed my son up for some sessions with Sherris. She was awesome—just what he needed. He has overcome his anxiety and is back acting like a normal teenager. He often listens to the recordings he made with Sherris. I cannot thank her enough."

—*Steve Duckhorn, Aurora, Illinois, USA*

"There are so many magical things I can say about Sherris, but I want to start off by saying how rare it is to find someone who truly cares and wants to see you improve. I went in trying to fix one thing, and Sherris helped me get down to the root of what was causing it, so we ended up fixing like six things! Did I mention she's also really funny, which helps? My advice to anyone seeking her help is to be open-minded and to trust her. The faster you do that, the quicker you'll see your life change."
—*Lauryn Johnson, Detroit, Michigan, USA*

The word "Psyche" means soul, and oh, how far has modern medicine come from integrating our soul or spirit into modern Psychology!? Sherris does a beautiful job of reintegrating our soul, spirit and essence back into transformational therapeutic work. She creates a compelling narrative for the power of hypnosis using science, story, and theory. If you're serious about working with your subconscious mind and integrating the physical and mental with the spiritual parts of you, this is a great place to start. Learn and apply these principles and notice how much better your life seems to get! NOW!
—*Nicholas Spohn, Speaker and Coach at the Ministry of the MindIowa, USA*

"The Peace of Mind Blueprint" is a powerful guide that offers a transformative approach to healing emotional and spiritual wounds through psycho-spiritual hypnosis. With compassion and expertise, the author provides readers with practical tools to achieve lasting peace, making this book an essential read for anyone seeking a profound shift in their mental and emotional well-being.
—*Susan Friedmann, CSP, international bestselling author of* Riches in Niches: How to Make it BIG in a Small Market

THE PEACE OF MIND BLUEPRINT

HOW TO STOP SUFFERING AND LIVE THE LIFE YOU TRULY WANT WITH PSYCHO-SPIRITUAL HYPNOSIS

SHERRIS COTTIER SHANK
ILLUSTRATOR LENA RUSH

The Peace of Mind Blueprint
How To Stop Suffering and
Live the Life You Truly Want
With Psycho-Spiritual Hypnosis

Copyright: Birmingham Clinical Hypnotherapy
ALL RIGHTS RESERVED

ISBN: 979-8-89079-141-2 (hardcover)
ISBN: 979-8-89079-142-9 (paperback)
ISBN: 979-8-89079-143-6 (ebook)

No part of this material or its associated ancillary materials may be reproduced or transmitted in any form or by any means, electronic or mechanical, including photocopying, recording, or by any informational storage or retrieval system, without permission from the publisher. For permission requests, contact Birmingham Clinical Hypnotherapy, 261 East Maple #203, Birmingham, MI, USA 48009

Legal and Earnings Disclaimer

While all attempts have been made to verify information provided in these materials and its ancillary materials, neither the author or publisher assumes any responsibility for errors, inaccuracies, or omissions, and is not responsible for any financial loss by the customer in any manner. Any slights of people or organizations are unintentional. If advice concerning legal or related matters is needed, the services of a qualified professional should be sought. The information contained in these materials is strictly for educational purposes. Therefore, if you wish to apply ideas contained in these materials, you are taking full responsibility for your actions. Neither the author nor publisher purport these materials as a "get rich scheme," and there is no guarantee, express or implied, that you will earn any money using the strategies, concepts, techniques, and ideas in these materials. Earning potential is entirely dependent on the efforts and skills of the person applying all or part of the strategies, concepts, techniques, and ideas contained in these course materials. Any examples, stories, or case studies are for illustrative purposes only and should not be interpreted as examples of what consumers can generally expect from these materials. No representations in any part of these materials are promises for actual performance. Any statements and strategies offered in these materials are simply opinion or experience, and thus should not be misinterpreted as promises, results, or guarantees (express or implied).

This material and its associated ancillary materials are not intended for use as a source of professional financial, accounting, legal, personal, or medical advice. You should be aware of the various laws governing business transactions or other business practices in your particular geographical location. The author and publisher disclaim any warranties (express or implied), merchantability, or fitness for any particular purpose. The author and publisher (Birmingham Clinical Hypnotherapy) or any of Sherris Cottier Shank's representatives shall in no way, event, or under any circumstances be held liable to any party (or any third party) for any direct, indirect, punitive, special, incidental, or other consequential damages arising directly or indirectly from any use of this material, which is provided "as is," and without warranties.

*For all sensitive
and inquiring souls,
I see you.*

Table of Contents

A Personal Note From Sherris xiii

Foreword xvii

Part One: The Power Of Psycho-Spiritual Hypnosis

Chapter 1 The Silent Crisis and the Invisible Wounds of Emotional Pain 3

Chapter 2 A Real Solution in a Time of Need 9

Chapter 3 New Hope for Those Who Have Tried It All. . . 17

Chapter 4 It's Time To Stop Suffering 22

Chapter 5 Trauma, Emotional and Spiritual Distress, Creativity, Performance, and Even Brain Surgery! 25

Chapter 6 The Biggest Myths About Hypnosis 35

Chapter 7 Embracing the Whole Mind: How
           Psycho-Spiritual Hypnosis Works........40

Chapter 8 Unlocking the Power of Your Subconscious
           Mind: Your Secret Ally in Personal
           Transformation 46

Chapter 9 The Most Important Things to
           Understand in This Book................51

Chapter 10 Your Subconscious Mind Runs Your Life ...53

Chapter 11 Big Wounds Require Big Change 60

Part Two: Befriending The Subconscious Mind

Chapter 12 Five Million Years Older.................75

Chapter 13 How To Talk to Your Subconscious Mind...84

Chapter 14 Why Does Change Feel So Hard? 98

Chapter 15 Making Change Easier 109

Part Three: Peace of Mind

Chapter 16 How to Have Peace of Mind............119

Chapter 17 The Power of Witnessing................129

Chapter 18 Emotional Messengers and
           Keeping Peace of Mind 139

Wrapping Up...................................149

A Personal Note From Sherris

Writing this book was a labor of love. It addresses the most frequent request I receive from clients: How can I achieve peace of mind? Clients want to live passionate, whole-hearted lives. They want to love freely and be loved in return, to understand themselves at the deepest level, and to live their lives in harmony and grace, free from haunting pain, fear, trauma, and self-sabotage.

If this is your quest, too, welcome! I am so glad you are here.

You will discover how psycho-spiritual hypnosis excels in healing seemingly intractable wounds by communicating with the subconscious mind, which runs in the background of all our lives and is the key to developing peace of mind. In addition, you will find stories from my life and from the lives of my clients that reveal the amazing truth about the power you hold inside.

Did you know that the subconscious mind is 90 percent of your mind or that all self-sabotage is a result of the conscious mind and the subconscious mind disagreeing? Were you aware that all your fears, traumas, memories, and creativity reside in your subconscious mind?

It's true! And the biggest surprise of all is that you can heal and resolve wounds that may have festered for years. That is exactly what happens in psycho-spiritual hypnosis.

If you've heard scary myths about hypnosis, I've written a whole chapter explaining how hypnosis works and why those myths are unfounded. I explain how your subconscious mind can become your strongest ally instead of your worst enemy and how you can find ease in fundamental change.

I also give you step-by-step directions on how to develop peace of mind in *your* life.

- Imagine finding a sanctuary of tranquility and serenity deep in your mind—a place of quiet detachment where you can see the whole picture and make decisions with ease.

- Imagine releasing, resolving, and healing invisible, emotional, or spiritual pain that has held you back for years.

- Imagine feeling the freedom and ease to follow the path *you* choose because it lights you up inside.

This is what is available to you when you embark on the path leading to peace of mind with psycho-spiritual hypnosis, and I would be delighted to be your guide.

THE PEACE OF MIND BLUEPRINT

Please reach out to me at ThePeaceOfMindBlueprint.com.

There, you can listen to the psycho-spiritual hypnosis recordings I offer in this book, set up an appointment to chat with me, or send me an email.

I would *love* to hear from you!

To your highest good,

Sherri

Foreword

In a world where many suffer in silence, battling emotional pain, inner turmoil, and a sense of powerlessness, Sherris Cottier Shank offers a beacon of hope by addressing invisible wounds and providing a path to healing that goes beyond symptom relief to address core issues in the subconscious mind.

Imagine waking each day not with a sense of dread but with a heart full of purpose and peace. This is more than a possibility; it is your potential reality, waiting to unfold with each chapter you explore in this wonderful book.

The Peace of Mind Blueprint: How To Stop Suffering and Live the Life You Truly Want with Psycho-Spiritual Hypnosis offers both inspiration and practical tools for creating the life you choose, free from the demands of others. Sherris's insights into the subconscious mind's transformative power reveal how true healing occurs, and her compassionate guidance empowers you to make positive choices that lead to a joyful life of deep peace.

I first met Sherris in March 2020 and felt an instant connection with her. Our initial conversation revealed her deep commitment to the well-being of others and her passion for making a positive impact in the world. Her sincerity and dedication were evident from the start, explaining why so many people are drawn to her and her work.

For the sensitive among us, every word in this book resonates with truth. You, who feel deeply and absorb everything around you with acute intensity, will discover here a powerful ally in your quest for serenity and self-realization.

In every story and example, Sherris shows you that in the quiet sanctuary of your mind, there exists a space untouched by noise and clutter: a place of pure potential and light. This book is your invitation to that sacred space. It is not merely a collection of pages but a journey into the deepest realms of your being, where true healing and profound transformation await.

The Peace of Mind Blueprint is a testament to Sherris's profound understanding of the human condition and her innovative approach to healing.

Through psycho-spiritual hypnosis, Sherris provides a powerful, drug-free method to alleviate emotional and spiritual pain, helping you create lasting peace of mind. Her approach is grounded in scientific research and extensive practical experience, making it both effective and accessible.

THE PEACE OF MIND BLUEPRINT

As you turn these pages, allow yourself to be guided not just by words but by the resonant energy they carry. Let this book be a mirror reflecting your light and darkness, a map leading you back to the essence of who you are.

Welcome to a journey of healing. Welcome to a future where you live not just in the world but truly within yourself—grounded, centered, and serene.

Welcome to *The Peace of Mind Blueprint*!

With heartfelt appreciation,
—*Kev Webster, Coach, Hypnotherapist, Author, and Teacher, Scunthorpe, England*

Part One

The Power Of Psycho-Spiritual Hypnosis

- From global crises and invisible emotional pain to unparalleled mental health and peace of mind, psycho-spiritual hypnosis is changing the world one person at a time.

- While most therapeutic approaches relieve symptoms, they don't change the core problems that remain stubbornly active in the deep inner mind.

- Psycho-spiritual hypnosis heals and resolves core wounds, so a transformation that looks impossible at first becomes ever more possible and probable.

- Psycho-spiritual hypnosis is a real solution in a time of great need.

Chapter 1

The Silent Crisis and the Invisible Wounds of Emotional Pain

"You're my last chance."

These were the words of a nineteen-year-old as he sat in my office.

Sadly, he was the first of many clients who informed me that I was their last chance. "I've tried everything," they say and go on to describe everything they've tried (unsuccessfully) to relieve their suffering: talk therapy, pharmaceutical drugs, street drugs, exercise, sports, psychics, etc. Everything helped a bit, but nothing fully relieved their emotional pain.

The truth is this young man is far from alone.

Did you know we are in a national and global mental health crisis?

- "Depression is one of the leading causes of disability. Suicide is the fourth leading cause of death among fifteen- to twenty-nine-year-olds. People with severe mental health conditions die prematurely—as much as two decades early—due to preventable physical conditions."
  —*World Health Organization*

- "Loneliness is far more than just a bad feeling—it harms both individual and societal health. It is associated with a greater risk of cardiovascular disease, dementia, stroke, depression, anxiety, and premature death."
  —*Dr. Vivek Murthy, United States Surgeon General*

- "US mental health is getting worse by multiple metrics. Suicide rates have risen by about 30 percent since 2000. Almost a third of US adults now report symptoms of either depression or anxiety, roughly three times as many as in 2019, and about one in two adults have a serious mental illness like bipolar disorder or schizophrenia."

—*Time Magazine*

But the mental health crisis isn't the whole story.

At the same time, we are experiencing a massive cultural movement toward holistic health, natural remedies, and alternative therapies for both physical and mental health. Particularly in the field of mental health, people are often looking for ways to resolve their distress without taking drugs.

Luckily, there is a method available to do exactly that.

You may have heard that line before, and you may have some natural skepticism; I totally get that. If you have invested hundreds or thousands of dollars and hours searching for solutions to emotional distress and/or behaviors you can't control, I understand your frustration. I, too, have walked that path.

If you're like most people, you may be dealing with one (or more) of the following:

- trauma
- depression
- anxiety
- panic attacks
- physical pain
- abuse
- low self-worth
- self-sabotage
- performance fear
- unhelpful ("bad") habits
- inability to move forward

- communication breakdown (professionally and/or personally)
- insomnia
- inability to focus
- procrastination
- addiction

The Invisible Wounds of Emotional Pain

Through my work assisting numerous clients in their healing and transformation journeys, my personal experience of transitioning from depression to sustainable confidence and contentment, and years of research, I have discovered one vital fact:

Most therapeutic approaches relieve symptoms but don't change the core problem that remains stubbornly active in the deep inner mind.

There is still a cauldron of sadness, fear, self-contempt, loneliness, and/or despair bubbling continuously beneath the surface, draining your energy, undermining your goals, and convincing you that you're powerless.

When this happens, it's easy to believe there's something "wrong" with you because the emotional pain that tears you apart on the inside is invisible from the outside. People who can't see your wounds may not understand why you feel so bad or how hard you have tried to escape the abyss you've fallen into.

This leads to feelings of never being good enough, never measuring up, and an inability to participate productively, which deepens your misery. When this goes on for months or years, the agony of feeling unseen and misunderstood takes a cruel toll on your sense of belonging in the social fabric of life.

It is so easy to feel alone.

But the good news is that you're not alone. I'm delighted for you to know that real, permanent change is not only possible but faster and easier than you ever imagined.

Now is the time when our world desperately needs this kind of help.

- Imagine how *your life* would change if you could heal those old wounds or remove the emotional obstacles holding you back.

- Imagine the impact if even 25 percent of the population healed the wounds that make them depressed, angry, anxious, powerless, or addicted.

- Imagine most people in our society being kind and compassionate because they were free of all the negative baggage they used to carry.

Our world would be a lot better, wouldn't it?
We could have this world now.

GEMS

Pause and reflect on these essential ideas.

- We are in a global mental health crisis.
- At the same time, there is an enormous desire for holistic treatments.
- Psycho-spiritual hypnosis offers a drug-free way to relieve emotional and spiritual pain so you can create peace of mind.
- You are not alone.

Chapter 2

A Real Solution in a Time of Need

In my search for peace of mind, I began by looking for ways to escape the pain of a deep depression that haunted my every step. I didn't know why I was depressed. I just wanted it to stop, believing that peace of mind would be on the other side of pain. I was driven to find a solution because I knew I wouldn't live very long if I stayed mired in the swamp of despair that was draining my life force.

That quest set me on a lifelong path of learning, growing, and becoming, resulting in changes I could not have imagined when I began.

Along the way, I collected tools to make the journey easier, and *hypnosis is by far the most potent tool* I have found for personal healing, growth, and expansion.

Not Just Any Kind of Hypnosis

Before we proceed, I want to clarify what hypnosis is, what it isn't, and the different forms of hypnosis available worldwide.

First, hypnosis is a naturally occurring state of consciousness (more on that later).

The experience of being in hypnosis is known as trance. While in a trance, you are neither fully awake nor fully asleep. You feel detached from your surroundings but can hear and communicate with a practitioner guiding you. You experience a heightened awareness of your deep inner mind and are more focused and receptive to suggestions.

This hypnotic experience can be used in many ways. Still, when most people hear the word hypnosis, they think about what they've seen on TV, in the movies, or on stage (i.e., entertainment). They need to be made aware of the therapeutic applications of this powerful tool.

Hypnosis for entertainment is called stage hypnosis. You've likely seen this: when a practitioner calls volunteers to the stage to be hypnotized and instructs them to do various (sometimes silly) things. People comply with these requests if they do not violate one of their core values.

The real power of hypnosis, however, is realized through its therapeutic capacities, helping people who are tired of suffering and ready to transform their pain into peace.

Clinical hypnosis (hypnotherapy) helps clients resolve emotional and psychological issues. It is used to heal trauma, fear, anxiety, self-doubt, low self-esteem, lack of confidence, phobias, feeling stuck in life, and other similar issues. Once the negative emotions are resolved, positive, empowering emotions are embraced. It is also effective in changing behavior and modifying unwanted habits.

This book is devoted to psycho-spiritual hypnosis that honors and embraces a person's emotional/psychological life and spiritual life. This is the most useful approach I've found for the hundreds of clients I've served.

Psycho-spiritual hypnosis includes all the emotional and behavioral healing of clinical hypnosis but also draws from a person's spiritual and existential experiences to enable the healing of core wounds and facilitate change. This approach inspires spiritual growth, self-awareness, and lasting transformation, often in a fraction of the time.

Hypnosis is effective for one simple reason: It allows you to tap the vast wealth of knowledge, talent, imagination, and intuitive knowing in your subconscious mind—the most significant, most powerful part of your mind.

According to *TIME Magazine*, hypnosis "has a surprisingly robust scientific framework. Clinical research has shown that it can help relieve pain and anxiety and aid smoking cessation, weight loss, and sleep. It can help children and adolescents better regulate their feelings and behaviors. Some people can even use 'self-hypnosis' to manage stress, cope with life's challenges, and improve their physical and emotional health."

My mission is to help you overcome the emotional, behavioral, and spiritual obstacles that prevent you from living as a fully empowered, sovereign person. A person who is free to choose the life you want, take joyful action to create it, and live with deep peace in your mind and joy in your heart.

This book is for you, especially if you want to:

- stop self-sabotage in its tracks
- get unstuck from an emotional, psychological, or spiritual obstacle
- leave behind negative habits that are holding you back
- stop living with a problem that you know you can't change without help
- become your truest, most natural, and authentic self

It is important to understand, however, that as fast and effective as psycho-spiritual hypnosis is, it is not a magic wand. It requires a committed and consistent approach as well as a deep desire to change your current lived experience.

You must show up with an open mind and a receptive heart to create the greatest change in the least amount of time.

You have to **WANT** to change.
You have to be **WILLING** to do the work.
You have to **VALUE** your growth so much that you dedicate resources—time, energy, and money—to your journey.

Throughout this book, you will see and experience what's possible as you open the door to real transformation.

When I work with clients, I focus on both their immediate challenge and their long-term goals. Focusing on their immediate challenge means guiding them through the best therapeutic processes to heal their specific inner wounds and/or conflicts. Focusing on their long-term goals means providing the emotional support, intellectual perspective, and/or spiritual view they need to sustain their journey.

I hope you find the inspiration, insight, and courage you need to face your inner wounds and conflicts as you read the stories of myself and others included on these pages. I also hope the information I provide about working with the subconscious mind gives you the perspective and support you need to persevere in your quest for peace of mind.

One great example is my client (whom I will call) Gwen, who overcame relentless, narcissistic abuse, regained her confidence and self-respect, and discovered a new, supportive relationship with a person who deeply values her company.

I'm delighted you've found your way to this book! I'm here to help you maximize your life experience for the greatest joy, love, satisfaction, and peace imaginable.

Where Have You Been All My Life?

When I discovered hypnosis, I wondered where it had been all my life. Why had it taken so long for me to find it?

Like many other people, I suffered through decades of depression, and just like my clients today, I searched far and wide for solutions. I embarked on years of talk therapy and spiritual counseling. I took antidepressants and researched endlessly. Over many years, I read or listened to every book, seminar, and presentation I could find on psychology, spirituality, and the brain. Everything I did helped, but nothing freed me completely from the abyss.

It took a massive medical crisis and fifteen months of astonishingly slow recovery for me to discover hypnosis. During that lengthy period of physical healing, there wasn't much I could do except read and sleep, and I had plenty of time to ponder the state of my life.

It was clear that I could not continue the way I had been, and my whole life needed to change. I asked myself repeatedly, "What does my soul want?" That extended recovery became a phenomenal blessing in disguise. It created space for the answer to that question to float up from my subconscious mind and allowed the more hidden aspects of my inner being to emerge. My deep spirituality rose to the surface, and with it came a longing to help others.

One day during my recovery, while idly surfing the Internet, I stumbled upon an article about hypnosis in *Psychology Today*. As I read it, something inside me lit up and stood at attention, and I felt compelled to learn more.

Have you ever had that experience when something grabs your attention and won't let go—when light bulbs start going off, and a tiny voice inside says, "Pay attention"? That's what I experienced as I read that article.

I had observed in the hospital that the medical community had only two things to offer me: drugs and surgery. Hypnosis appeared to be an alternative healing modality that could help me relax and accept what was happening to me so I could adapt to my physical needs.

The more I explored, the more I wanted to know, and my thirst for knowledge about hypnosis grew at every step. I read every article and book on the subject and researched places where I might study further. As soon as I was well enough, I enrolled in a training program at the Clinical Hypnosis Institute and discovered the tool I'd been looking for my whole life.

I was in heaven.

Now, having worked with hundreds of clients, I am writing this book to bring holistic, emotionally healing psycho-spiritual hypnosis to a wider audience.

It's time to stop suffering.

GEMS

Pause and reflect on these essential ideas.

- The experience of being in hypnosis is known as trance, where you are neither fully awake nor fully asleep.

- Psycho-spiritual hypnosis encompasses the emotional and behavioral healing provided by clinical hypnosis while integrating a person's spiritual and existential experiences to heal core wounds and facilitate change

- To create peace of mind, you have to **WANT** to change. You have to be **WILLING** to do the work. You have to **VALUE** your growth so much that you dedicate resources—time, energy, and money—to your journey.

- It's time to stop suffering.

Chapter 3

New Hope for Those Who Have Tried It All

Imagine you are looking for shipwrecked treasure at the bottom of the ocean. The ocean is vast and deep, but after years of effort, you finally locate the shipwreck, and all you have to do is reach the bottom to retrieve the treasure.

You try diving, but even with the most sophisticated, up-to-date equipment available, the ocean floor is miles too deep for you to reach. You try a submarine especially built for this trip, but that, too, turns back when the pressure of the deep ocean threatens to tear the submarine apart. Then, one day, you remember something you read in all the old sailing stories you researched, a method of reaching the bottom of the ocean used by ancient seafarers.

Most of the modern world dismisses this ancient method as a myth, a tall tale that can't possibly work. It's too easy, they say; you'll die trying. However, the more you think about it, the more it makes sense to you, and you take a leap of faith and decide to try this technique and see what happens.

Much to your surprise and delight, you quickly reach the treasure and bring it to the surface. This ancient method succeeds easily and quickly, and you are amazed. After a lifetime of searching and struggling, you have claimed the treasure and changed your life.

This is how it feels when you solve a long-festering problem by simply relaxing into hypnosis and efficiently communicating with your subconscious mind. It feels like a miracle, and you are so glad you took that leap of faith and explored this healing modality that's been waiting for you all this time.

When I discovered hypnosis, it was like stumbling on the holy grail: the secret to profound, lasting personal change that I had searched for my entire life. The more I learned about it, the more excited I became. Here was a modality with the power to radically change my life—a healing modality unequaled in powerful, drug-free, holistic mental health care.

According to Dr. David Spiegel, Associate Chair of Psychiatry at Stanford University, hypnosis has been "used for more than two centuries to treat a host of medical problems, particularly pain management and anxiety… now available to patients at some of the most respected medical institutions in the country, including Stanford Hospital, the Cleveland Clinic, Mount Sinai Medical Center, and Beth Israel Medical Center in New York."

Michael Yapko, Ph.D., Clinical Psychologist, teaches us that "the hypnotic state allows for a focused concentration and heightened suggestibility, which can be utilized to facilitate behavior change and reduce symptoms of anxiety, depression, and chronic pain."

What these quotes don't tell you is *why* hypnosis is so effective. The reason is hiding in plain sight.

- Most emotional, psychological, and spiritual problems *live in the subconscious part of the mind.*

- Most therapeutic modalities approach emotional, psychological, and behavioral problems using *only the conscious mind.*

- *The conscious mind has no access to the subconscious mind*, so clinicians and clients often end up circling the problem but never reaching the core wound causing the distress.

- With hypnosis, you can go directly to the cause of the problem in the subconscious mind, heal the original wound, and create the vision and expectation of a new, preferred reality.
- Like my client, whom I will call Natalie, who found the courage to leave a relationship she knew would never grow into the partnership she craved, reclaim her self-worth, and develop a genuine belief in herself.

GEMS

Pause and reflect on these essential ideas.

- It feels like a miracle when you solve a long-festering problem by simply relaxing into hypnosis and efficiently communicating with your subconscious mind.
- Hypnosis is now available to patients at some of the most respected medical institutions in the country.
- With hypnosis, you can go directly to the cause of the problem in the subconscious mind, heal the original wound, and create the vision and expectation of a new, preferred reality.

Chapter 4

It's Time To Stop Suffering

What you'll find in this book is a clear description of how your mind works and how you can heal your emotional and spiritual wounds with psycho-spiritual hypnosis so you can create a life of peace and joy.

Most therapeutic protocols approach emotional and spiritual healing through the conscious mind. Unfortunately, the blocks to your emotional and spiritual wellness are not in your conscious mind. They are in your subconscious mind.

The great power of psycho-spiritual hypnosis is its ability to communicate directly with your subconscious mind and address the core wound or problem causing your distress. Once the core wound is healed, you change and evolve naturally and easily because your subconscious mind sends you different signals and messages.

(I've not only helped individuals but also rooms full of people at business conferences.)

The following pages also contain abundant information about the power of your subconscious mind. Your subconscious mind is 90 percent of your mind; without access to it, you are profoundly limited in your ability to heal and resolve the issues holding you back.

I've arranged this book in an easy-to-follow discussion that begins with an in-depth explanation of psycho-spiritual hypnosis, how it has helped my clients and me, and a description of the many kinds of problems that can be solved with its use.

I have also included information about the subconscious mind to help you better understand its function and importance.

You will read stories about my healing as well as those of a few of my clients so you can understand the depth of change that is possible with psycho-spiritual hypnosis.

Finally, there is a discussion of peace of mind itself, what it is, what it is not, and what it is like to live with a foundation of well-being that supports the peace of mind you seek.

You can skip to different sections, but the information will make the most sense if you start at the beginning and read to the end.

Chapter 5

Trauma, Emotional and Spiritual Distress, Creativity, Performance, and Even Brain Surgery!

Much of my work revolves around helping clients heal and resolve trauma and emotional or spiritual distress. People come in for many reasons, including persistent anxiety, depression, a bad breakup, a sudden occurrence they can't get over, relationship issues, procrastination, a feeling of being trapped or stuck, or a frightening medical diagnosis. Some simply can't stand being tortured by their thoughts anymore.

The one thing all these people have in common is they are suffering from invisible pain that is derailing their lives, and they want the pain to stop—now. They want peace of mind.

Remember the nineteen-year-old who told me I was his last chance? He was traumatized by an experience that frightened and humiliated him. When he tried traditional therapy and found no relief, he told his dad that he'd like to try hypnosis, and at their next meeting, his psychiatrist referred him to me.

When we began working together, he refused to attend classes or talk to anyone outside his immediate family. As we healed and deactivated the original trauma, which greatly relieved his distress, he began to get comfortable being around people again. After a few more sessions, where we worked on rebuilding his sense of safety and confidence, he was back at school and working a part-time job.

This is the power of dealing directly with the source of the wound in the subconscious mind. Once the wound is healed, the subconscious mind sends different signals—the signals for fear and humiliation stop, and the signals for comfort and safety resume.

Celebrities also turn to hypnosis for trauma recovery and personal growth.

- **Martha Stewart** used hypnosis to overcome nightmares following her release from jail.
- **Jackie Kennedy Onassis** used hypnosis to relive and let go of the tragic events in her life.
- **Princess Diana**, the late Princess of Wales, reportedly used hypnosis to overcome the trauma and emotional pain of her highly publicized divorce from Prince Charles.

It is difficult to overstate the relief you feel after healing a long-festering emotional wound. Thoughts that haunted you stop, and panic attacks disappear. But most of all, you feel a new hope and optimism that propels you to a future that suddenly looks friendly and welcoming again.

Befriending your subconscious mind is the best decision you will ever make.

Overcoming Performance Fears

People are stalked by performance fears in various endeavors, including sports, business, music, public speaking, writing, and the arts. Any time you stretch beyond the familiar into new and uncertain territory, you are susceptible to performance fears. Self-doubt suddenly runs rampant, and you begin to wonder why you ever wanted this thing in the first place.

This happens because the subconscious mind wants to protect you, and from its vantage point, anything unknown looks unsafe. The fear signals are meant to hold you back from something dangerous. At this point, clients tell me things like, "I am my own worst enemy," or, "I don't know what's wrong with me."

There's nothing wrong with them; they must let their subconscious mind know that what they want isn't dangerous and is highly desirable. This is done by communicating to the subconscious mind:

- specific, measurable goals that turn the unknown into the known
- a clear vision of success and all the steps to create it
- determination and desire to succeed
- the benefits of achieving their goal
- the joy they will feel when they accomplish this goal

When coupled with repeated hypnotic rehearsals and reinforcement of the client's strengths and talents, the subconscious mind starts to look for ways to help create the achievement they're looking for. This process is so reliably productive that hypnosis has become the secret weapon of many successful athletes and actors.

Athletes use hypnosis to heighten concentration and focus despite distractions, to block out pain, and to visualize success.

- **Steve Hooker** (pole vaulting) won the 2008 gold medal after using hypnosis to visualize his success.

- **Mary Lou Retton** (gymnastics) used hypnosis to block pain in her foot and won the gold medal for gymnastics.

- **Tiger Woods** (golf) began seeing a hypnotist at the age of thirteen to help him block out distractions and focus on the game.

- **Andre Agassi** (tennis) worked with **Tony Robbins**, utilizing NLP and hypnosis.

- **Jack Nicklaus** (golf) attributes his success in golf to hypnosis and visualization techniques

Many actors also use hypnosis to create confidence and visualize their roles.

- **Lily Tomlin** worked with the great Hollywood hypnotherapist Gil Boyne and loved hypnosis, saying, "If I had my own company, everyone would be required to listen to Gil Boyne's tapes every day."

- **Sylvester Stallone** turned his acting career around by working with Gil Boyne before filming *Rocky*.

- **Matt Damon** said, "Using hypnosis was one of the greatest decisions of my life."

- Other actors who use hypnosis include **James Earl Jones, Bruce Willis, Tony Curtis, Demi Moore, Julia Roberts,** and **Orlando Bloom.**

Stimulating Creative Thought

Scientists, writers, and creatives of all sorts use psycho-spiritual hypnosis to generate ideas and alternative solutions that the conscious mind might immediately reject.

- **Carl Jung and Sigmund Freud** developed modern psychiatry as a result of learning about and practicing hypnosis.

- **Wolfgang Amadeus Mozart** (1756–1791) apparently composed the famous opera *Cosi fan Tutte* while hypnotized.

- **Albert Einstein** (1879–1955), a physicist, was known to go into a trance through self-hypnosis every afternoon. His theory of relativity came to him during one of these sessions. He also used trance states to develop his ideas.

- **Lord Alfred Tennyson** (1809–1892) wrote complete poems while hypnotized.

- **Thomas Edison** used self-hypnosis regularly.

- **Aldous Huxley** used trance-like states to explore the nature of consciousness.

- **Sergei Rachmaninoff** (1873–1943) reputedly composed one of his concertos following a post-hypnotic suggestion.

If you desire this sort of creative thought, I would be happy to teach you self-hypnosis so you can access this inspired state of mind daily. Make sure to connect with me at

ThePeaceOfMindBlueprint.com so you can start creating the life you want.

Hypnosis for Brain Surgery?

Really?

Hypnosis allows surgeons to get reliable, real-time responses from a patient during deep brain surgery. When using anesthesia, the effects of the sedatives distort results, but with hypno-sedation, that is not a problem. As a result, the surgery is more accurate and effective.

> "Surgeons have completed the world's first deep brain surgery using hypnosis instead of an anesthetic to control the patient's pain. Doctors carried out the deep brain stimulation procedure to cure the seventy-three-year-old patient's severe trembling hands. The seventy-three-year-old patient from Thuringia, Germany, whose tremor did not adequately improve with medication, is reportedly very satisfied with the result of the six-hour operation by the team from the University Hospital of Jena."
> —*Acupuncture and Wellness Center of Florida*

Hypnosis and Saving Lives

In 2013, French firefighters began training in medical hypnosis to soothe trauma victims who might be trapped under rubble, in a car following a crash, or even having an asthma attack. Firefighters use hypnosis to divert the victim's attention away from the trauma so they may be treated more easily.

According to EMS1.com, station manager David Ernenwein says, "The first thing that we can do to help people is to calm them down, and this technique has given us the tools to be able to do that, to help people suffer less."

Relieving Physical Pain

Hypnosis is also used medically to reduce pain around the world.

France is among many nations that have adopted this practice, using hypnosis to block pain during cancer treatments and even during heart surgery. Hypnosis is less invasive than other protocols and enhances the other care being given.

Julie Mayon, training and scientific director at the Institut Français d'Hypnose (IFH) in Paris, said: "Hypnosis can make treatments less uncomfortable, as well as reducing pain and anxiety. Long term, it can give people a more positive memory of their hospital stay, and the reduction in anxiety helps people recover better, sleep better, and experience less chronic pain, which improves overall quality of life."

While it is more widely accepted in Europe than in the US, hypnosis is now available to patients at some of the most respected American medical institutions, including Stanford Hospital, the Cleveland Clinic, Mount Sinai Medical Center, and Beth Israel Medical Center in New York.

So, what does all this mean for you?

When it comes right down to it, does it matter that hypnosis has helped all these people?

It only matters if there is something you want to change, accomplish, or grow in your life that would benefit from activating the incredible power of your subconscious mind. The real value of hypnosis is that you employ your whole mind, not just your conscious mind.

We can't solve problems with the same thinking we used to create them.

Albert Einstein believed that ingenious thought was triggered by allowing the imagination to float freely, forming associations at will, and this is exactly where the subconscious mind excels. He used hypnosis to stimulate ideas and solve problems, *and you can do that, too!*

If your problems are rooted in trauma, psycho-spiritual hypnosis can help you.

If your problems are rooted in performance, psycho-spiritual hypnosis can help you.

If your problems are rooted in visualizing the best possible future for you, psycho-spiritual hypnosis can help you.

Psycho-spiritual hypnosis is a legitimate and easily accessible tool for transformation. How far you go with it is your choice. As a psycho-spiritual hypnotherapist, it is my job to create the conditions that allow you to do the work you want to do.

So, what do you want? What have you been unable to resolve?

To quote Einstein one more time, "We cannot solve our problems with the same thinking we used to create them." We *can* solve our problems by accessing the much more expansive thinking of the subconscious mind.

Psycho-spiritual hypnosis allows you to quickly change your perspective, see things from a more detached state of mind, resolve emotional traumas, and create new opportunities. It is a potent tool that will work for you just as it has worked for many others. It's been an honor to see such wonderful outcomes for my clients firsthand.

GEMS

Pause and reflect on these essential ideas.

- The great power of hypnosis is the ability to heal emotional and spiritual wounds directly in the subconscious mind. Once the wound is healed, the subconscious mind sends different signals—the signals for fear and humiliation stop, and the signals for comfort and safety resume.
- Many athletes and actors use hypnosis to increase performance.
- Hypnosis is also used medically, including as hypnosedation for brain surgery.
- Albert Einstein used hypnosis to stimulate creative thought.
- "We cannot solve our problems with the same thinking we used to create them." We *can* solve our problems by accessing the much more expansive thinking of the subconscious mind.

Chapter 6

The Biggest Myths About Hypnosis

Although many psychiatrists, psychologists, social workers, and therapists use hypnosis in their practices today, it is still a protocol shrouded in mystery for most people, and myths abound.

When you know the truth and debunk the myths, you are empowered to decide whether hypnosis is right for you based on your needs and opinions.

Myth #1 – A hypnotist will "make me" do things I don't want to do.

Some people first encounter hypnosis as a stage act that is designed to entertain. This, unfortunately, creates a fear that a hypnotherapist will make them bark like a dog or quack like a duck, and that fear creates a preliminary distrust.

All I can tell you is that as an active psycho-spiritual hypnotherapist, I have zero desire to embarrass or threaten you. My goal is always to help you free yourself from whatever is holding you back, and I don't waste your time or mine in such antics.

Myth #2 – I can't be hypnotized.

Hypnosis will work for you *if you want it to. Your attitude is the single most vital factor determining your success* in hypnotherapy.

People who have experienced hypnosis before or who have a personal meditation practice can usually relax into the hypnotic state with ease. People with anxious, racing minds sometimes have difficulty initially, but extra relaxation work accommodates that.

The subconscious mind speaks in images, symbols, stories, body sensations, emotions, repetition, and metaphors. It is important to trust what your subconscious mind shows you during hypnosis. There is plenty of time afterward to analyze your experience with your rational, conscious mind.

Myth #3 – I won't remember anything, and I won't know what happened.

Just as it is easy to forget your dreams, it can be easy to forget what happens in hypnosis. In my practice, I record all hypnosis sessions and ask you to listen to them again between sessions. This accomplishes two things: You have a record of everything we do during hypnosis, and when you listen to the recording between sessions, you deepen your subconscious mind's understanding and acceptance of your healing.

Myth #4 – Hypnosis isn't safe.

People often ask me about the side effects of hypnosis. Will they be too sleepy to drive? Will they feel hungover? Will they awaken demons that get out of control?

The answer to all these questions is an emphatic no.

Hypnosis feels like a deep, guided meditation. When it's over, you feel relaxed and awake—and likely better than you've felt in quite some time.

Myth #5 – I will lose control of my mind.

This is the biggest myth of all, and nothing could be further from the truth. In reality, you gain control because you can communicate directly with your subconscious mind.

When I work with clients, I am the guide; they take the journey and do the work. They *allow me* to guide them into a deeply relaxed hypnotic state so that together, we can work to resolve the identified problem. While their conscious mind hears and observes everything in this relaxed state, it isn't dominant. They can discuss what happened and consciously process their insights when brought out of the hypnotic state.

The actual experience of psycho-spiritual hypnosis dispels all the myths surrounding it.

Personally, I find hypnosis to be like a very lucid dream. During the process, I can hear everything that is being said, respond to questions, and easily retrieve information. I feel safe, comfortable, and somewhat detached from my body and surroundings, yet I can tune in on a much deeper level. It's an enjoyable experience where I can visualize and understand information quickly.

GEMS

Pause and reflect on these essential ideas.

- Many psychiatrists, psychologists, social workers, and therapists use hypnosis in their practices today.
- Stage hypnosis is entertainment.
- Psycho-spiritual hypnosis enables emotional and spiritual healing.
- Hypnosis feels like a guided meditation or lucid dreaming. When it's over, you feel relaxed and awake—and likely better than you've felt in quite some time.
- Hypnosis is safe. The client is always in control.

Chapter 7

Embracing the Whole Mind: How Psycho-Spiritual Hypnosis Works

Psycho-spiritual hypnosis helps create the conditions and environment that allow you to *choose the life you wish to live, free from any past conditioning.* People face endless hurdles when doing change work independently and can end up feeling stuck with no idea how to move forward.

Negative emotions and unproductive beliefs that have persisted for years keep them imprisoned in their old thoughts and behaviors. When guided through hypnotic change, those negative emotions and unproductive beliefs can be specifically addressed, dissolved, and replaced with helpful and positive emotions and beliefs.

It's important to understand that emotional and spiritual obstacles that take root over time are stored in the subconscious mind, triggering bad feelings in the present. They may have started years or decades earlier as an event that was too painful to process at the time.

As years pass, those feelings can grow and fester until they turn into what might be described as an emotional abscess. The cure for that abscess is guided, focused attention *without interference from the conscious mind.*

The conscious mind means well, but it can be a bit of a bully. After all, solving problems is one of its primary jobs, and when it can't solve a specific issue, it tends to run in circles, descend into overthinking, and interfere where it doesn't belong.

- The conscious mind is dominant in our daily lives, and the subconscious mind runs in the background.

- In hypnosis, the subconscious mind becomes dominant, while the conscious mind is in the background.

- When the subconscious mind is dominant, a person can focus solely on the core wound and solve problems that may have haunted them for a lifetime.

I tell my clients to imagine the subconscious mind like a field they want to clear and prepare to grow a new crop. In this endeavor, you are clearing an internal, subconscious field where you can plant the intentions, thoughts, and feelings that create the life you desire.

If you were clearing a physical field and planting new crops, your first job would be to remove the big rocks that are taking up valuable space and preventing tender new roots from taking hold.

The big rocks in your subconscious mind are traumatic experiences and emotional wounds waiting to be healed.

These big rocks suck up valuable mental and emotional energy and prevent you from experiencing the peace that is the foundation for pursuing your dreams.

In psycho-spiritual hypnosis, you start by removing the big rocks. You heal the wounds draining your energy and leaving you feeling powerless.

The second step in clearing a physical field is to till the earth, remove all the little rocks, break up crusted soil, and loosen the dirt so new roots can grow and expand. The little rocks and crusted soil in your subconscious mind are the toxic beliefs you've collected along the way and voices of criticism and belittlement that become loud and debilitating if left unchecked.

Loosening the soil in the field of your mind is the adoption of new empowering beliefs and the positive mind training that prepares your subconscious mind to embrace your new vision.

Then, you plant. You choose the vision that lights you up, makes your heart sing, and effortlessly pulls you forward. This is your true calling, finally audible and visible to you now that the ground has been prepared and the obstacles removed.

To activate this vision, you embrace new patterns of thought that you practice daily and create a new emotional setpoint that you step into easily after removing emotional burdens.

After planting, you nurture. You continue your positive mind training to neutralize any opposing thoughts or criticisms that pop up and distract you from your strong intent to build a life you love.

So, how can you know if psycho-spiritual hypnosis will help you?

Allow yourself some quiet time for self-reflection and ask these questions:

- Am I struggling with negative emotions that I can't resolve?
- Am I emotionally or physically drained because of a nagging fear, worry, or depression?
- Is there an issue from the past that I can't make peace with?
- Am I feeling lost and just surviving day-to-day?
- Am I living in around-the-clock fight or flight?
- Do I lack the confidence to live the life I want to live?

- Is there something stealing my happiness that I can't name?
- Do I feel out of control and consumed by chaos?
- Is there a person in my life whose negative influence is so great I can't escape their grip?
- Do I need help?

If you answered yes to any of these questions, psycho-spiritual hypnosis can help you.

Being in a deeply relaxed state of hypnosis, or trance, is a healing experience. Deep within us, there is a place of peace and tranquility, an inner sanctuary that we can tap into, and psycho-spiritual hypnosis enables you to experience this. Allowing yourself to drift into a hypnotic trance soothes your nervous system, which allows you to viscerally experience the sensation of being safe, secure, and at peace. *When was the last time you felt safe, secure, and at peace?*

Here's the truth: You don't have to allow emotional burdens to drain your energy and block your future, and you don't have to live with that invisible pain forever. It comes down to a choice.

GEMS

Pause and reflect on these essential ideas.

- When guided through hypnotic change, negative emotions and unproductive beliefs are specifically addressed, dissolved, and replaced with helpful and positive emotions and beliefs.

- Imagine the subconscious mind like a field you want to clear and prepare to grow a new crop. In this endeavor, you are clearing an internal, subconscious field where you can plant the intentions, thoughts, and feelings that create the life you desire.

- Allowing yourself to drift into a hypnotic trance soothes your nervous system, which enables you to viscerally experience the sensation of being safe, secure, and at peace.

- You don't have to allow emotional burdens to drain your energy and block your future, and you don't have to live with that invisible pain forever. It comes down to a choice.

- On the other side of pain is freedom and spaciousness.

Chapter 8

Unlocking the Power of Your Subconscious Mind: Your Secret Ally in Personal Transformation

Nothing is more exhilarating than watching someone release trauma, overcome fear, and stand their ground as the magnificent being they are. Every time I witness this in a client, it is more thrilling than the last, and my passion for psycho-spiritual hypnosis and personal transformation grows a little more.

My clients often experience a series of epiphanies and turnarounds as they begin deactivating painful experiences festering in their subconscious minds. I have seen the transformation possible when a person is truly ready to embrace change, and it is thrilling to watch. When a person can no longer tolerate being consumed by an endless cycle of negative thoughts and turbulent emotions and is ready to embrace psycho-spiritual hypnosis, they can resolve and release old wounds quickly and step into the wholeness of who they are.

Emily's Story

One such client, whom I will call Emily, was grieving the death of a daughter she had aborted under duress. She was very young at the time of the pregnancy. She wanted to keep the child, but her new husband vehemently objected. Without support from other family members, she faced an impossible decision with no good alternatives.

Years later, while working with me, she shared her belief that she deserved punishment for getting that abortion, and she could not forgive herself, even though she now had healthy children at home. Her guilt gnawed relentlessly at her self-respect and sense of self-worth. She felt cursed for life and could see no way out.

As we worked together, I had the strong intuition that Emily needed to talk to that daughter, who was now in Spirit and ask for her forgiveness. This would be impossible for the conscious mind, but the subconscious mind has no sense of time or space and talking to people in Spirit is no different than talking to people who are flesh and blood.

During that hypnotic conversation, Emily apologized to her child and told her the name she had picked for her. She asked for and received forgiveness and was able to give and receive deep love. The results were miraculous.

When Emily arrived for our next session, she told me that for the first time since that event occurred so many years earlier, she felt a deep sense of peace with what happened and a 100 percent reduction in guilt.

A transformation that looks impossible at first becomes ever more possible—and probable—as emotional roadblocks are eliminated one by one, creating the space for confidence and enthusiasm to grow.

When someone says to me, "I can't stand this. I can't live like this anymore," I throw up my hands in celebration and say, "Wonderful! You're in the perfect place for change." At that point, we become partners in a life-affirming journey of healing and growth, and I can't think of anything that fires me up more.

I often tell clients that they drive the bus, and I navigate. They tell me where they want to go, and I find the fastest, easiest route. This sums up the collaborative journey of psycho-spiritual hypnosis: There's a place you want to reach, and the hypnotic process that gets you there. It's a step-by-step process, with one session building on another until, one day, you realize, "Hey! I'm not filled with angst and pain anymore."

And *that* is a beautiful discovery!

GEMS

Pause and reflect on these essential ideas.

- Clients often experience a series of epiphanies and turnarounds as they begin deactivating painful experiences festering in their subconscious minds.

- A transformation that looks impossible at first becomes ever more possible—and probable—as emotional roadblocks are eliminated one by one, creating the space for confidence and enthusiasm to grow.

Chapter 9

The Most Important Things to Understand in This Book

Human beings tend to complicate things. I know I certainly do! So, without any complication, here are the core ideas in this book.

1. Your subconscious mind runs your life.
2. If you want peace of mind, you must heal the hidden and invisible wounds in your subconscious mind.
3. You must want peace of mind with every fiber of your being and be willing to do the work to produce it.
4. When you heal the wounds and release the toxic or debilitating beliefs in your subconscious mind, you can adopt new positive, supportive beliefs that fuel peace and joy.
5. Once you have established peace of mind, you must nurture it with ongoing attention to what you think and feel to prevent backsliding into old familiar habits.
6. You can live without constant angst, trauma, and worry if you choose to.

If you remember nothing else, these ideas will serve your highest good.

Chapter 10

Your Subconscious Mind Runs Your Life

"**No one skates.**"

Those are my late husband's words, commenting that no matter who you are, you inevitably encounter challenging circumstances and painful lessons that require you to change and adapt. How you handle those experiences either derails you from your goals or propels you to your desired outcome.

Sooner or later, you trip over the truth that life is about learning how to live successfully. Living successfully means learning how to live the life *you want*, regardless of circumstances, and learning to be the person *you* want to be without interference from other people's beliefs and demands.

In short, this means learning how to allow your soul to soar while managing the "business" of living.

This requires change—significant change, constant change. Life always throws you a new challenge, and if you resist change, you doom yourself to misery or stagnation.

However, it doesn't have to be that way. You have a powerful silent partner working in the background that can be your best friend and ally or a constant impediment to growth, and that partner is your subconscious mind.

Did you know that your subconscious mind runs your life?

It's true. The conscious mind, while powerful, is no match for the bigger, older, more potent subconscious mind because that is where all your fears and beliefs live.

It's pretty good at "self-sabotage."

Here's why: No matter how much you consciously plan and work toward the change you want—or how much willpower you apply—a contradicting fear or belief in your subconscious mind will stop you every time. After expending a lot of effort, you eventually realize that you can't muscle your way through a specific problem, achieve a specific goal, or shake a destructive feeling, and repeated attempts are immune to your efforts. Nothing will happen until that fear is released or that belief is altered.

This is the cause of all "self-sabotage."

Have you ever done something and then wondered, "Why did I do that?"

Have you ever kicked yourself for allowing a golden opportunity to pass by because something held you back?

Have you ever wondered why you can't speak your truth?

The answers to those questions, and many more, are in your subconscious mind.

And here's another truth: Your subconscious mind *wants* to help you. It stops you from doing things because it believes it is protecting you from harm. Somewhere in the past, it learned that certain things are dangerous and should be avoided. Until it unlearns those things, it will do everything it can to protect you from them.

If you have a burning desire to accomplish important goals, to love without remorse, and to embrace all that life has to offer, it would be wise to communicate with your subconscious mind, and there is no better way to do that than through hypnotherapy.

Here's an example from my life.

I was almost finished with my hypnotherapy classes and was designing the website for my business when I ran into a fear that stopped me in my tracks. I kept stumbling over the feeling that anything I wrote would be misunderstood for reasons I could not explain. When I expressed this in class, the instructor, Cheryl Beshada, asked if I'd like to investigate that fear, and I enthusiastically said yes.

After guiding me into hypnosis, Cheryl asked my subconscious mind to search for the original cause, and it turned out to be an event that occurred when I was eight years old. I saw an image of myself sitting on my bunk bed at camp, night after night, printing letters to my parents on the small, scented, blue writing paper bought especially for this purpose. Every letter said the same thing. "Dear Mom and Dad, I hate this camp. The counselor is mean. Please come and take me home." Every day, I mailed a new letter.

When I first saw that image, I couldn't believe it and immediately thought, *Oh, that can't possibly be it!* As soon as that thought appeared in my mind, the image got bigger and more detailed, and I realized this was the cause of a fear that was crippling my self-expression. I was dumbfounded.

When my parents didn't come to take me home, my little girl brain decided it must have been because I had not written my request clearly. Why else wouldn't they come? I convinced myself that my writing was misunderstood.

This is the power of the subconscious mind: An innocent childhood experience and a false belief stored forever in my deep subconscious mind created fear around everything I wrote. Once this was uncovered, it was easy to heal and let go. Problem solved.

To create the life and profession I wanted to create, I had to release an old fear that was blocking my way forward. If I had not released that fear, I might never have finished my website or written this book, and my disappointment would have nagged me forever.

Some fears and beliefs take a little more digging and a bit more courage to release because to become one thing, you have to unbecome something else.

To step into the new life your heart and soul desire, you have to step out of the old life that isn't fulfilling you.

To soar, you have to leave the safety of the ground.

GEMS

Pause and reflect on these essential ideas.

- Life always throws you a new challenge, and if you resist change, you doom yourself to misery or stagnation.

- No matter how much you consciously plan and work toward the change you want—or how much willpower you apply—a contradicting fear or belief in your subconscious mind will stop you every time.

- If you have a burning desire to accomplish important goals, to love without remorse, and to embrace all that life has to offer, it would be wise to communicate with your subconscious mind, and there is no better way to do that than through hypnotherapy.

- To become one thing, you have to unbecome something else, and your subconscious mind is the key to that change.

An Invitation

One of the most significant wounds most people live with is an inability to love themselves and a lack of self-compassion.

If this is you, it's not your fault. There's nothing wrong with you. No one teaches us how to love ourselves. Often, we are taught that to love ourselves is bad, egotistical, or arrogant. It's not. Loving ourselves is the foundation of all emotional well-being.

The good news is there's a short, simple way to cultivate more love and self-compassion.

Visit ThePeaceOfMindBlueprint.com/recordings right now for a soothing five-minute audio recording on self-compassion. Listen to it daily to really build your self-compassion muscle.

The more you listen, the better you'll feel. Enjoy!

Chapter 11

Big Wounds Require Big Change

My world shattered when my husband died of esophageal cancer.

Mike was my soul mate, lover, best friend, and safety in the world. We were so much alike that I could sense what he was feeling from across a crowded room, and he could do the same for me. I knew every expression that ever crossed his face and could instantly feel if something was wrong. I trusted him absolutely. Living without him never crossed my mind until the day the doctors told us his cancer was terminal.

I did not take this news well.

Indeed, I fought their pronouncement with every ounce of energy I had. I endlessly researched treatments that could help him. As I watched Mike descend into the hell of chemotherapy and radiation, I demanded that the doctors come up with a solution. I became obsessed with saving Mike from this fate. I couldn't lose him! I couldn't! Going on without him was unthinkable, and I refused to accept that possibility.

A Quick History

When we got married, I was twenty-six, and Mike was thirty-two. Finding him was the greatest joy of my life. He was tall and handsome, and his easy laugh was infectious. He loved to hike, dance, and play Frisbee and had an encyclopedic knowledge of the things that interested him most: jazz, books, and films. He could name the directors and actors of hundreds of films and all the musicians in the many recordings he loved and admired.

Most of all, Mike loved me. He saw me for exactly who I was and loved what he saw. There was no pretense between us. We fit together perfectly in every way. We both felt like outsiders in a world that was often mystifying, but when we were together, everything made sense. We both hated fighting and found other ways to work things out. We agreed, for instance, that the person who cooks, cooks his or her way, and the other person is a respectful and tolerant helper. There were no fights, and there was no back-seat cooking. It worked for us.

Neither of us fit into the corporate world, and we both chose careers creating beauty. Mike loved fine woodwork and devoted himself to cabinet finishing and antique restoration. I embarked on a career as a goldsmith and eventually turned to gemstone carving.

Mike was legally blind in one eye, which was a blessing. It gave him excellent color sense because color was all he could see through his bad eye. Whenever he wanted to judge true color, he closed his good eye and looked through his bad eye. He was the best judge of the myriad variations of color I ever knew and a great help to me when judging gemstones.

The Discovery of Cancer

The cancer was discovered accidentally when the doctors were looking for something else, and it was already at an advanced stage four when they found it. In fact, they initially found it in his liver, where it had metastasized, and it took over a month to find the original tumor in his esophagus. Twenty percent of patients with stage four metastasized esophageal cancer survive for one year or more. The oncologist told us that with treatment, Mike might live for another year, without treatment, six months.

We were lucky; Mike lived for two years after his diagnosis, giving both of us the space and time we needed to accept what was happening. Mike needed to accept that his life would end far earlier than he had imagined, and I needed to accept how powerless I was to stop the outcome of his disease.

For a year, I researched relentlessly, looking for alternative treatments. I was on every list of esophageal cancer patients I could find. Time after time, I brought him a new treatment to consider, and he would smile kindly and say, "I'm not interested in that."

Undaunted, I went back to my research and looked again and again until one day, I realized, *Oh, he's not interested in any new treatment.* Mike was tired. It took every bit of his energy to get from one day to the next with the treatment he was doing. He didn't have the available life force to take on anything else.

Tumors in the Brain

One night, he showed me a new lump in his neck that was causing him pain, and we rushed to the emergency room. It turned out to be a blood clot caused by the chemotherapy he was receiving, and before the ER doctor could treat it, he had to get an MRI of his brain. That's when the news got really bad. The cancer had spread to his brain.

They radiated his brain repeatedly with both general and site-specific radiation. For the site-specific treatment, they used a metal cage to hold his head still. They screwed that cage into his skull with metal screws while he was awake and without pain meds that would disrupt the outcome. This is considered very advanced medicine, and I am sure it is, but to me, it looked barbaric. Mike never complained.

The seizures started without warning. One night, he started shaking and fell off the couch, unable to control his body. He was terrified, and I had no idea what to do for him. His sister Nora, a nurse practitioner, raced to our aid, giving me instructions over the phone about how to hold his head and what to look for as she drove to our house.

After that, Mike was in and out of the emergency room with seizures regularly and was sometimes hospitalized for days before they would release him. I remember driving him home from one of those extended stays. He was looking out the passenger side window, and I wondered what he was thinking. Then, he turned his head, looked at me, and said, "Thanks for driving, hon." It was all I could do not to burst into tears.

Mike didn't remember that he hadn't driven for months or even appear to know why we were in the car. All he knew was that he was in the car with me, and I was driving, and he was glad. Even after enduring multiple brain seizures and repeated radiation, his kind and loving personality was still intact.

To this day, I am grateful for that. His core personality never altered. He couldn't tell whether it was day or night and asked me the same questions repeatedly because he couldn't remember the answers, but the essential Mike was still present. No matter what else he lost, the man I fell in love with remained true to himself until the very end.

Dying and the Aftermath

Mike died in my arms, in our home, surrounded by family, two years and one month after his diagnosis. He'd been under hospice care for several weeks and kept in a morphine coma to prevent seizures. They'd stopped all other therapeutic medicine, and I'm pretty sure a blood clot hit his heart. His eyes suddenly popped wide open, and he turned to look at me. For about sixty seconds, we stared into each other's eyes while I said over and over, "You're so beautiful. You're so beautiful."

Then, he was gone.

The shock of realizing he was gone was impossible to process. How could this man I loved so much suddenly not be there? How was that possible? The ability to focus my eyes vanished. I could barely hear, and the room felt like it was moving. Nothing made sense to me; my mind seemed to be broken. So much of my world ended when Mike left his body, and I was in no way prepared.

For the two years of his illness, every thought I had began and ended with Mike. I stopped working and devoted myself entirely to his care. We never talked about what my life would be like after his death because he couldn't stand the pain that caused him, and I was unwilling to make his life any more difficult than it already was. There was only one thing I cared about—helping Mike. Every minute of every day was focused on what he needed.

When Mike died, my life was suddenly empty. Not only was the man I loved most in the world gone, but my reason for living was also gone because he was no longer there for me to care for. Nothing mattered anymore. I stumbled through a memorial with friends' and family's generous and dedicated help and went home to an empty house.

I stopped opening mail and paying bills, which led to the gas company threatening to cut off my gas three times. It wasn't that I didn't have the money; it was just that paying the gas bill felt meaningless and irrelevant. Why did the whole world insist on moving forward when my entire world had collapsed?

Friends and family were kind and tried to help me, but I was utterly lost. I was a walking shadow of the person I used to be, and the world felt foreign and dangerous. I wondered why I was there. I went to bed every night for a year and a half, begging Mike to come and get me. All I knew was I wanted the pain to stop and dying and joining Mike was the only path I could see.

Mike often came to me in my dreams, but he never took me with him. No matter how hard I begged, I was still there in the morning. After about eighteen months, I stopped asking. Little did I know that my repeated death mantra would come back to haunt me.

Fight, Flight, and More

We are closest to our subconscious mind right before falling asleep and just as we wake up. I went to sleep every night begging Mike to come and get me and woke up every morning disappointed that he hadn't, and that rooted my desire to die deep into my subconscious mind.

As time went on, I managed to pull my life together again, and it was close to a decade later when I began to feel waves of burning pain in my esophagus. Isn't it interesting that the pain I felt was in the same place where Mike's tumor was lodged? There are no coincidences in this world.

The pain came and went, and I mostly felt annoyed. It was a nuisance. I took over-the-counter heartburn medication and carried on with my life. Over a couple of months, the waves of pain became more frequent and intense until it felt like my esophagus was on fire. I would brace myself against the wall, praying for the pain to stop, and carry large bottles of liquid antacid everywhere I went.

You may wonder why I didn't see a doctor. I know that when I look back on this time, I certainly wonder why. The answer lies in how the subconscious mind works. In a crisis, we are catapulted into fight or flight, like I was every time the pain roared back to life again. When we are in fight or flight, the capacity of our prefrontal cortex, where all our rational thinking happens, is suppressed, and the subconscious mind signals us urgently to fight, run away, or hide.

I hid.

Unable to think straight as the pain became unbearable, I eventually found myself crawling across the floor to knock my phone off an end table. I called my oldest friend and hoarsely croaked a single word: "Abbie." That was all it took. The next thing I knew, I was in an ambulance on the way to the hospital.

As you may have guessed, I was having a heart attack. Afterward, the surgeon said wryly, "You waited a little long."

It's true. I didn't know I was having a heart attack and my rational mind was being suppressed. If I had known I was having a heart attack, I would have gone to the hospital earlier. As it was, they put in a stent and sent me home in four days.

Hospitalized on a Ventilator and an Epiphany

One month later, almost to the day, I was in an ambulance again because there was blood in my stool. My intestines tied themselves in a knot and were threatening to rupture. Luckily, I got to the hospital in time and happened to draw the chief surgeon who was on call that night.

All went well until I began to bleed through the nose because the resident scraped my esophagus while putting a tube down my nose and into my stomach. I woke up on a ventilator.

Being on a ventilator while conscious was horrendous. I had no control over my breathing, and my arms were tied to the side of the bed to prevent me from ripping it out, which I most certainly would have done. The doctors would not remove it until they were positive I could breathe on my own. I'm sure they were aware of my rage and distress, but their job was to keep me alive, and that meant staying on the ventilator for several more hours.

I was in the hospital for nine days. As I lay in bed at night staring at the ceiling, I asked myself over and over, "What is causing this massive breakdown in my body?" After pondering this question for days and nights on end, the answer came to me: I had asked for it. I had asked to die. I had prayed to die continuously for a year and a half, and my subconscious mind didn't know there was a time limit on that request.

Yes, there was a real blockage in my artery. Yes, my intestines did tie themselves in a knot. The physical causes were real. They were delayed because it took time for my subconscious to deliver on my request. When it did, I was given two possible ways out of this world, and I didn't take either one.

Seeking Peace of Mind

Why? Why didn't I take the opportunity to die when it was presented to me? All I had to do was lie down and let it happen.

I came to understand that what I actually wanted was peace. After Mike died, the only peace I could see was following him and dying, too. Years later, when these two maladies struck, I was beginning to embrace the possibility of healing. I was starting to believe I could survive without Mike and build a life worth living. I was beginning to understand that there was still work I wanted to do in the world, and I wasn't ready to die after all. I just never updated my subconscious mind.

This is why it is so important to communicate clearly with the subconscious mind.

If hypnotherapy had been available to me during my grieving process, I might have avoided those physical issues. However, I did not know it existed. I did not know that I was rooting the desire to die in my subconscious mind. I did not know that I could re-educate my subconscious mind as my desires evolved.

Now, I do, and I want you to know, too.

As I look back on that time, I realize there were many truths I couldn't face. I couldn't face the fact that Mike was going to die, and there was absolutely nothing I could do to stop it. I couldn't accept that I was alive and Mike wasn't. Somehow, I had to find a way to live and thrive without him.

Most importantly, I couldn't face the truth that my thoughts and desires were so powerful that they could cause a heart attack or worse.

I literally programmed myself to die.

Remember that old saying, "Be careful what you wish for because you just might get it"? That saying has potent truth, and now, you know why. When your thoughts and desires take root in your subconscious mind, it will do everything possible to make them come true. *This is true for both positive and harmful desires.* It's up to you to know what you want, to choose wisely, and to keep your subconscious mind updated as your desires evolve.

Your mind is far more powerful than you were taught to believe. When your conscious and subconscious minds work in harmony, you can manifest dreams at a rapid rate. Psycho-spiritual hypnotherapy is the tool that can help you accomplish that.

GEMS

Pause and reflect on these essential ideas.

- By repeating my death mantra over and over for eighteen months, I programmed myself to die.
- It took time for my subconscious mind to create the conditions in my body to accomplish that desire, and by that time, I wanted to continue living.
- It's up to you to know what you want, to choose wisely, and to keep your subconscious mind updated as your desires evolve.

Part Two

Befriending The Subconscious Mind

- The subconscious mind runs your life, and it's important to remember that it is neither modern nor rational.
- It speaks its own ancient language and functions according to its own ancient rules.
- When you learn to communicate with your subconscious mind, change becomes surprisingly fast and easy because your subconscious mind wants to help you, and all it needs is up-to-date information.
- By collaborating with your subconscious mind, change feels so natural that you begin to feel you've always been this new way.

Chapter 12

Five Million Years Older

Would you be surprised to learn that the subconscious mind is five million years older than the conscious mind? This surprises the heck out of my clients.

In a 2013 *Scientific American* article, Professor John Hawkes explains that the human brain has tripled in size in the past seven million years. Most of this growth happened in the last two million years, when the prefrontal cortex developed, the area of the brain responsible for conscious thought and rational analysis. Before that time, humans had only the subconscious mind.

The subconscious mind is a highly evolved and ancient creature that has been developing for over seven million years. It is guided by its own intuition and knowledge and has been operating that way for eons. It may have an awareness of the conscious mind, but unless it receives new information in a language it understands, it has no reason to change its course.

With its five-million-year head start, the subconscious mind had plenty of time to develop most of the traits that still influence our lives today. For instance, its number one priority is keeping us alive, and it has an incredible ability to regulate our bodies, including the power to shut down organs. This is evident in the final stages of life when individuals often stop eating because their subconscious mind has deactivated their digestive system, allocating energy to the heart and lungs, which are vital for survival.

Another crucial role of the subconscious mind is to protect us. It remains ever-vigilant, constantly alert to signs of danger, ensuring our safety even when we're consciously unaware of any imminent threat. Without this trait, early humans could easily be killed and devoured by animals that were bigger and stronger than they were. The individuals who survived were constantly aware of threats from the outside, and that facility still flourishes today.

The immensity of the difference between the subconscious and conscious mind becomes even more apparent when you consider the amount of information each processes.

Did you know the conscious mind can only process forty pieces of information per second?

That's a small number compared to the eleven million pieces of information the subconscious mind receives and processes every second.

Imagine processing eleven million bits of information per second consciously. It would quickly become impossible, and we would likely go crazy or stop functioning. Luckily, our subconscious mind processes all the information our conscious mind can't handle, allowing us to function effectively without becoming overwhelmed.

The conscious mind is a problem solver and mistakenly believes it is in control.

Our individual minds reflect our evolutionary process as we mature. We are born with a vast subconscious mind, but our conscious mind only begins to appear sometime between the ages of five and seven. Even then, it is a slow, gradual process to a fully developed conscious mind that does not occur until our early twenties.

During the first five years of life, we live entirely in our subconscious mind. This means that as young children, we absorb all the information, suggestions, and circumstances around us without the ability to analyze them.

Consequently, we tend to accept what we are told as truth. Many of our beliefs are formed during those first five years when we lack rational thinking skills. If some of those beliefs become unhelpful later in life, the quickest and easiest way to change them is to re-educate our subconscious mind, and there's no better way to do that than through psycho-spiritual hypnotherapy.

In truth, both our conscious and subconscious minds are required to function effectively and harmoniously, but their respective limitations can impede this.

The conscious mind is a problem solver and mistakenly believes it is in control. It is unaware that it is continuously responding to information processed by the subconscious mind and cannot operate without this information.

On the other hand, the subconscious mind does not realize that its conclusions about an event or experience may not be accurate. It reacts quickly, instinctively, and defensively and requires the conscious mind's careful, considered judgment to balance it.

Where Self-Sabotage Begins

When the subconscious and conscious minds disagree, the subconscious mind wins every single time because it possesses all the power. This is precisely why willpower, defined as the strong determination to achieve something challenging, can sometimes fail. Willpower is a feature of the conscious mind and can be overridden if the subconscious mind perceives a threat.

As a problem solver, the conscious mind is constantly analyzing, questioning, and planning and can become a bit of a bully in pursuing its desired outcome.

This is a bit like a very intelligent scuba diver trying to exert his dominance over a great blue whale. The whale goes on about its business regardless of what the scuba diver thinks. The scuba diver may have more rational abilities, education, and better analytical skills than the whale, but the whale is uninterested in those abilities and carries on as it always has.

Take, for example, the desire to lose weight. I have worked with people who have tried every diet and exercise program available. Some have even had gastric bypass surgery, but the weight they lose always returns. Besides producing a sense of fatalistic despair, the constant cycle of gaining and losing weight can lead to even more significant physical challenges.

Why, then, do these very motivated people run into trouble? The simple answer is that their subconscious mind believes they need the weight, and once that belief is changed, they will be able to achieve their goal.

Mary's Story

When my client, whom I'll call Mary, came to see me, she had tried everything. Her weight embarrassed and angered her because she could not understand it.

She was the oldest of six children and was raised in a strict religious household. Her family moved both within and outside the country several times during her childhood. She was rarely in a school longer than a year and did not make friends easily. She was now married with children of her own but still felt utterly alone.

Although she appeared to be competent and in control on the surface, there was a fragility about Mary. She talked too fast, and she found it difficult to look at me directly. Her thoughts wandered wildly when I asked specific questions, and her hands were always moving.

To calm her, we did some gentle hypnosis work around self-empowerment and self-compassion, and as she began to trust me as her guide, we began asking her subconscious mind direct questions.

In what turned out to be her breakthrough session, I asked Mary's subconscious mind if being overweight served any worthwhile purpose in her current life. The reply was, "Yes."

"What purpose does it serve?" I asked.

In the soft, mumbled voice that many people use during hypnosis, Mary said, "Keep people away."

I repeated this to confirm I had heard it correctly, and Mary said, "Yes."

When I asked what people needed to be kept away, I knew Mary was seeing something behind her closed eyes because she began to cry and shake her head as if denying the image in her mind. When I asked her to describe what she saw, she could only say, "Father in bed."

I sensed Mary did not want to see anymore at that moment, so I suggested she watch as that image gradually became smaller and smaller, shrank to the size of a dot, and then disappeared. When the image was gone and Mary was again peaceful, I brought her out of hypnosis.

As we talked about what she saw, Mary looked perplexed. "I thought I was over that," she said. At a young age, Mary intentionally closed off that experience with the intent of never thinking about it again. She didn't discuss it with anyone, including her husband.

Nonetheless, those memories of sexual abuse were stored in her subconscious mind and had now morphed into a festering wound that needed to be healed. Until Mary resolved this, her subconscious mind would continue to keep her safe with excess weight that made her feel unattractive.

Healing Invisible Wounds with Psycho-Spiritual Hypnosis

Not everyone's story is as dramatic as Mary's. There are countless reasons why the subconscious mind might believe a person needs excess weight to protect them. I have worked with highly sensitive people who can't process all the feelings they absorb from others, so their subconscious mind stores them in the body.

Some people believe they are too unimportant to warrant good self-care. Others fear they won't belong anymore because everyone in their family is overweight. Thankfully, we don't have to guess the reasons because the subconscious mind knows the answer. It's just a matter of asking.

After the shock of her discovery, Mary quickly progressed in regaining her mental and physical health. Through several sessions of hypnosis, I guided her to release the trauma she experienced, express her deep rage and grief, deactivate her shame, and reassert her power to control her life.

At that point, she could share with her subconscious mind that she was safe now and no longer required the extra weight to protect her. She was ready to let it go. After all those years of burying that trauma in her body, Mary was free to focus on the much simpler work of changing her diet and exercise habits, allowing the weight to dissolve and disappear slowly.

This is the power of the subconscious mind in action. You may consciously want something desperately, but if the subconscious mind sees that desired outcome as a threat or a danger, it will throw up obstacle after obstacle to prevent it from happening as it endeavors to protect you.

By talking directly to the subconscious mind in hypnosis, you can work with it instead of against it. You befriend your subconscious mind by respecting its power and mission to protect you and communicating your current desires clearly and honestly. In this way, your subconscious mind becomes your best friend and strongest ally instead of your constant impediment.

You are the only person who can do this work, but you don't have to do it alone. Clients often confide in me, saying, "I am my own worst enemy," and I am delighted to inform them that we can work together to deactivate this self-sabotaging pattern and achieve their goals.

GEMS

Pause and reflect on these essential ideas.

- The subconscious mind is a highly evolved and ancient creature that has been developing for over seven million years and is five million years older than the conscious mind.
- The top priorities of the subconscious mind are to keep you alive and protect you.
- Willpower is a feature of the conscious mind and can be overridden if the subconscious mind perceives a threat.
- You befriend your subconscious mind by respecting its power and mission to protect you and by communicating your current desires clearly and honestly.

Chapter 13

How To Talk to Your Subconscious Mind

Step One: Access the Subconscious Mind

As you go about your daily life, the conscious mind is dominant, and the subconscious mind is in the background. In psycho-spiritual hypnosis, these roles are reversed, so the subconscious mind becomes dominant, and the conscious mind assumes a watching and listening role.

Relaxing is the easiest way to access the power of your subconscious mind. As you relax, your brainwaves get longer and slower, unlocking the door to your subconscious mind. This is why most psycho-spiritual hypnosis sessions begin with relaxation.

A brainwave is a measurable and recognizable pattern of electrical impulses in the brain. Five brainwaves—delta, theta, alpha, beta, and gamma—have been measured and identified in humans.

Human beings move back and forth between different brainwave states all day long. Sleeping (delta), daydreaming (alpha or theta), and being wide awake in full concentration (beta) are all examples of brainwave states.

About the Brainwave States

Beta brainwaves dominate most of your day-to-day life. In this state, you are firmly in the conscious mind and actively engaged in mental activities such as reading, speaking, thinking, or calculation. It is interesting to note that staying in a beta wave state for too long leads to feeling overwhelmed and stressed. When you relax, you change your brainwave state and alleviate those sensations.

A person who is awake and thinking but relaxed and not actively solving a problem is likely in an alpha brainwave. This might occur when a person is so deeply involved in a project that they forget about time, when taking a break and enjoying a sunny garden, or just having a good time with friends.

Alpha brainwaves are the bridge between your conscious and subconscious mind and are the birthplace of the "Eureka" moment when new ideas arise spontaneously out of nowhere. Those ideas come from the subconscious mind that suddenly has access to you.

For instance, I move into an alpha brainwave every time I take a long hot shower. As I enjoy the hot water and my body relaxes, my subconscious mind can suddenly give me the answers to problems I'm trying to solve or supply ideas for the creative project I'm engaged in. I love this—what an incredible added benefit to showering!

As you prepare to sleep and once again as you wake up, your brainwaves slow down and become longer. During this state, known as the **theta brainwave state,** your subconscious mind is dominant. Theta brainwaves are present when you are not fully asleep or awake and when you are asleep and experiencing vivid dreams.

Theta brainwaves are believed to occur even when you are awake. If you find yourself lost in a vivid daydream, you are likely experiencing theta brainwaves. Similarly, if you are driving and suddenly realize that you can't recall the last fifty miles because you were lost in thought, it's also probable you were in a theta brainwave state. Your intuition and creativity greatly increase when you are in a theta brainwave state.

During psycho-spiritual hypnosis, people are usually floating between an alpha and theta brainwave state, so it is easy to talk to their subconscious mind.

During sleep, our brain activity shifts into the longest and slowest brainwave, known as a **delta brainwave state**, where the subconscious mind is entirely dominant. Delta waves have the slowest frequency and the highest amplitude among the five different brainwave states humans can experience.

Gamma brainwaves are less thoroughly understood in neuroscience but are known to be important in learning, memory, and processing. They generally connote complex operations and sharp concentration.

Step Two: Speak the Language of Your Subconscious Mind

Your conscious and subconscious minds work differently. When we talk about thinking, we usually refer to the activity of the conscious mind, which is focused on solving problems in a linear and future-oriented way. Words and numbers are the preferred languages of the conscious mind, and its thoughts revolve around past, present, and future events.

On the other hand, the subconscious mind focuses on the underlying meanings of words and events. It exists only in the present moment and has no concept of time. It archives emotionally processed memories and events, and those memories and events that have not been emotionally processed persist and cause problems. Mary's story is an excellent example of how such memories fester until healed.

After years of research and analysis by numerous experts, we now know that the main languages of the subconscious mind are:

- storytelling
- metaphors
- emotions
- body sensations
- symbols
- images
- repetition

This makes sense when you consider that throughout most of human history, verbal communication was the primary method of transmitting knowledge. This is why storytelling, metaphors, emotions, body sensations, symbols, images, and repetition became so important. These same elements helped ancient humans remember necessary information and made it easy to pass that information down from generation to generation.

The subconscious mind's language is as old as humanity itself—an enduring connection to our primal roots.

Hypnotic Language

Hypnotic language is designed to appeal to both the conscious and subconscious minds. It utilizes words that the conscious mind can analyze while presenting in the subconscious mind's preferred languages.

For example, I was recently invited to lead a group hypnosis session at a three-day business conference. The CEO's goal for this session was to help the attendees begin their conference journey feeling "calm, confident, open, and teachable."

Notice that the CEO did not ask me to help the attendees think a certain way. The request was to help them *feel* deep inner comfort, serenity, self-confidence, and a willingness to learn.

To accomplish this goal, I created a process that would allow each goal to evolve naturally. First, I wrote an introduction to help the attendees relax into an alpha/theta brainwave state so I could communicate with their subconscious mind.

In the therapeutic part of the process, I lead the listeners on a journey to the library of their subconscious mind and give them an opportunity to explore all the treasures there. Some treasures resolved old wounds, and others sparked an enthusiasm to learn.

Meeting the Wise Woman

We gathered in the yoga room of the resort hotel where the conference was held. Each person had a yoga mat with bolsters and blankets so they could arrange themselves in a comfortable, semi-reclined position.

To begin the journey, I asked them to close their eyes and imagine taking a long walk through a mystical forest. I included images to engage them through body sensations:

> As you walk along the winding path, a slight breeze brushes your skin, and you hear birds singing in the trees—birds you recognize and birds that are new to you.

> There is a pervasive sense of peace, calm, and safety here, and you know deep in your core that there is something special about this forest as a wave of serenity washes over you. Something deep inside you stands down and surrenders to the tranquil waves of relief flowing through you right now.

I then encouraged them to lean into the experience with enticing details like,

> For reasons you can't explain, you begin to collect things, such as small branches, particularly attractive stones, a feather you find on the trail, and treasures from your walk.
>
> It's been such a long time since you've strolled and collected small treasures anywhere that the little kid in you suddenly wakes up and wonders what else you might find.
>
> Remember that little kid you used to be—the one who loves to discover new things in the world, find secret places no one else has ever seen, maybe even create a hidden getaway from the rest of the world.
>
> That little kid is still alive inside you and is opening your heart and soul to the awe of the forest as your whole body responds with alert attentiveness. And then you find yourself spontaneously running and laughing with the sheer joy of being alive and embracing this magical place with your entire being.

Even at this early juncture, this process incorporates story, body sensations, emotions, and images so the subconscious mind is engaged right from the very beginning.

Now, it is time to bring in metaphor and symbolism in the form of a wise woman,

Then, you see it. It's a small cabin perched on a hill. Stopping to look and survey the possibilities, you realize that sitting outside the cabin, next to a small fire, is an old woman with a rugged, open, and friendly face.

You remember all the tales you used to hear about the Wise Women who live in these woods, and you walk slowly toward her to see how she might react.

When the listener bravely asks the Wise Woman, "*What will set my heart at ease?*" She surprisingly directs them to the library.

This story confuses the conscious mind. First, they're in a forest, and then encounter a wise woman who directs them to a library. A library in the forest makes no sense, prompting their conscious mind to disengage even further.

However, their subconscious mind exists beyond the constraints of time and space, and to it, this story is entirely plausible and fascinating.

At this point, everyone in the room was relaxed and engaged, so the real work of helping them feel open and willing to learn could begin. It's time to enter their subconscious library.

When they walk through the large wooden door that magically appears in the forest, they find,

An astonishing room designed specifically for you. It's large and open, with all the lights, furniture, and art that are perfect for you—and the books! The books are amazing!

Long shelves of books extend in rows from two walls. On one wall are books that contain all the memories of your life. Good

memories and less-than-good memories are all stored here, waiting for your perusal. The rows are arranged by decade, one long row for each decade of your life. And you notice there are many rows still waiting to be filled.

This entire section of the process is designed to bring the listener calm and peace by allowing them to peruse good and not-so-good memories and decide whether they want to keep or release them. Because they are in a hypnotic trance, they feel detached from the usual emotional reactivity that might accompany those memories, and they can make a clear and easy choice. This takes a fair amount of time as several memories are examined from different periods of their lives.

The subconscious mind presents the memories the listener is ready to release, and the story incorporates a dramatic and permanent way for them to accomplish that.

Peace and calm emerge from the listener's relief in letting go.

Now, it's time to encourage confidence and a willingness to learn.

Now, turn your attention to the long rows of shelves on the other wall. These shelves hold the books on all your personal qualities, gifts, and talents. Today, we are looking for one particular book. But before we search for that one book, wander through these rows and begin to peruse all your amazing personal qualities, gifts, and talents. There are so many of them! Some you recognize. Some may surprise you. Allow yourself to be amazed and delighted at what you find. Bask in this knowing of your immense talents and capabilities.

Who wouldn't want to look at books that enumerate their gifts and talents?

How incredibly exciting! The subconscious mind shows them traits they did not realize were gifts or talents, heightening their delight at the discovery.

Then, to their surprise, they discover books that most people don't know exist.

> *Then, make your way to the row labeled "Superpowers." Yes, superpowers, your superpowers. Let that sink in. Your superpowers. There are books here you will want to return to, but right now, we are looking for the one titled* Curiosity.
>
> *What? Curiosity is a superpower? Oh, it most certainly is. In curiosity, you are emotionally balanced, neither in despair nor ecstasy. You are simply open, available, interested, enthusiastic, and alert—the perfect combination of emotions for learning, growing, and success.*
>
> *Find the giant, heavy volume titled* Curiosity *and carry it to the nearest table. This book is far too large to look at while standing. There are long wooden tables in the center of the room for you to use, so pick the one closest to you, take a seat, and set the* Curiosity *book on the table.*

Once the listener finds the huge volume that details everything they've ever been curious about, from birth to the present moment, they have several tasks to complete. By delving into their interests and fascinations, they reignite their fascination with learning and are prompted to decide what interests them most in their current life.

When they return the *Curiosity* volume to the shelf, they discover a book titled *Change* that holds the greatest secret of all: a method to unlock resistance to all forward movement.

After they discover the *Change* book and its secret, the process is complete, and all the original goals for the session have been achieved. There is some winding down and getting comfortable with everything they've discovered, and then I gently and slowly bring them out of hypnosis. After stretching and getting comfortable again, we all enjoyed discussing what they experienced.

Notice how this hypnotic process used all the languages of the subconscious mind: storytelling, metaphors, emotions, body sensations, symbols, images, and repetition. The repetition is most challenging to see through this brief description but happens through repeated visions of memories and repeated suggestions to dive deep, discover, and explore.

This is how hypnotic language engages the subconscious mind, encouraging it to shift its perspective and gain a new understanding of how to navigate daily life's many problems, decisions, and events.

• • •

Here's the revised text: If you want to tap into the calm, tranquility, and problem-solving abilities of your subconscious mind, let go of old memories that no longer serve you, and uncover your hidden gifts, talents, and superpowers, please listen to the recording of *"Your Subconscious Library"* at ThePeaceOfMindBlueprint.com/recordings

Set aside forty-five minutes when you can relax in a private place where you will be undisturbed. Choose a semi-reclined position that supports your neck and give yourself permission to experience the transformative effect of sinking into your subconscious mind

Access *Your Subconscious Library* at ThePeaceOfMindBlueprint.com/recordings

GEMS

Pause and reflect on these essential ideas.

- Relaxing is the easiest way to access the power of your subconscious mind. As you relax, your brainwaves get longer and slower, unlocking the door to your subconscious mind.

- The language of the subconscious mind is as old as humanity itself—an enduring connection to our primal roots.

- Hypnotic language is designed to appeal to both the conscious and the subconscious mind. It utilizes words that the conscious mind can analyze while presenting them in the preferred languages of the subconscious mind.

- In the hypnotic process described above, listeners go on a journey to the library of their subconscious mind and have an opportunity to explore all the treasures there. Some treasures resolved old wounds, and others sparked an enthusiasm to learn.

"Without Sherris and the therapeutic hypnosis session, the impact of our event would have been less profound. Sherris truly enhanced the quality of our conference. I am passionate about therapeutic hypnosis and wanted to share its transformative power in a live session with our event participants. On the morning of day two, Sherris led a subconscious library process that allowed our participants to effortlessly address and release something that may have been difficult for them. This experience opened their minds, hearts, and souls to a deeper and more intimate understanding of our work together. Sherris adeptly addressed curiosity and change, bypassed conscious resistance, and guided our participants to experience change in a new way."

—*Madeleine MacRae, CEO of Legacy Leadership Institute*

Chapter 14

Why Does Change Feel So Hard?

The urge to write a book began to form in my mind several years before I started writing this one. In fact, I had active dreams about writing a book before I had my first conscious thought about it. These were not pleasant, happy dreams; they were more like mini nightmares.

In each dream, I would attempt to sit down at a computer to write, but something would happen that prevented me from doing it. The chair would break, a co-worker would steal my computer, the electricity would go out, or the floor would start to rumble and roll.

In one dream, I was on the USS Enterprise Spaceship from *Star Trek*, and my desk was directly beside the antimatter warp drive. As I approached the desk, the warp drive started to malfunction, loud alarms went off, and I had to evacuate.

Looking back, it's clear that my dreams reflected a deep inner fear about writing a book. At the time, I found these dreams to be curious but failed to register the importance of the fear they were communicating. Had I worked with that fear then, I might have saved myself a lot of time and frustration.

Eventually, I mustered up the courage to start writing, but it was a slow and laborious process. I felt like I was wading through mud, as nothing seemed to come naturally. I struggled to find the right words and create an interesting narrative. Whenever I attempted to write, I would get overwhelmed by the sea of information that seemed impossible to organize. I knew the information I had to share was valuable and important, but I couldn't express it clearly.

Despite having a skilled coach to guide me, my mind hindered progress every step of the way. I persisted for almost a year but eventually gave up in frustration. I'd written thousands of words but was no closer to a book than when I started.

When I was processing my disappointment over my perceived failure at book writing, I found myself repeatedly asking, "Why is this so hard?" I grew up in a family of writers. Both my parents were reporters in their younger days. I wrote for the student newspaper in college and continued to write in various capacities throughout my life. *How*, I wondered, over and over, *could this be so hard?*

The answer is simple once you see it. It is so simple that it is easy to look right at it and radically underestimate its impact.

The subconscious mind equates familiarity with safety, causing everything unknown to become automatically dangerous.

I feel compelled to say that again because it is so simple and so important.

The subconscious mind equates familiarity with safety, causing everything unknown to become automatically dangerous.

In its relentless pursuit to protect you, the subconscious mind perpetually scans for potential threats. Remember that old saying, "Better the devil you know than the devil you don't"? That might be the guiding principle of the subconscious mind and is the core reason behind the belief so many of us carry that change is hard.

Change feels hard because the subconscious mind believes you are putting yourself in danger every time you step out of the familiar and into the unknown.

In my *Star Trek* dream, the danger was presented as life-threatening. I found this perplexing and wondered for a long time why my subconscious mind could possibly consider writing a book to be life-threatening. Then, in one of those sudden aha moments, I realized it had to be a fear of judgment.

Now, you might ask why a fear of judgment would be life-threatening, and that would be a reasonable question. From a modern, rational point of view, being judged negatively might be uncomfortable, disappointing, or distressing, but it is certainly not life-threatening.

It's important to remember that the subconscious mind is neither modern nor rational.

It is rooted in our most primitive development as a species when negative judgment from the dominant group could be life-threatening. In ancient times, a negative judgment might result in being banished, ostracized, and permanently cut off from the safety and support of the community on which you depend.

For me, publishing a book created the possibility of widespread negative judgment from my society, and that possibility triggered a primal fear. When I saw and understood this, it helped me in two ways.

First, I was clear in my rational mind that negative judgment wouldn't kill me, and I communicated this information to my subconscious mind through self-hypnosis, repeatedly reinforcing the belief that writing a book is safe and appropriate.

Second, I renewed my awareness *and respect* for how differently the conscious and subconscious minds view potential threats and learned again to stop and question the fear I was feeling before making decisions or embarking on a project.

Like many people, I used to ignore my fear and force myself forward, believing that I could achieve success solely through willpower. That's exactly what I did the first time I tried to write a book. In hindsight, I now realize that this approach is horribly inefficient and a waste of valuable time and energy. My subconscious mind is immensely more powerful than my conscious willpower and will stop me at every turn if I persist in blindly pressing onward.

For you and me, it is far better to stop and ask, "Why am I feeling fear?" The reason for the fear might not be obvious at first, and it might take you a while to discover it. However, taking the time to determine if this is simply something unknown and therefore frightening to the subconscious mind or a real threat that you need to pay attention to can help you make an informed decision about your next steps.

Unfortunately, none of us are trained to communicate with our subconscious mind and include it in our plans so we can benefit from its power. In fact, in Western society, we are taught that rational thinking is supreme and that our fears should be conquered and overcome. I grew up believing this, and it is likely you did, too.

Imagine how much easier it would be to cooperate and collaborate with your subconscious mind instead of struggling against it at every turn. Imagine tapping into the vast resources of the other 90 percent of your mind and using them to achieve the future you desire.

The Comfortable Lure of the Familiar

Dependence on the familiar is rooted in ancient survival instincts and reinforced during early childhood when the subconscious mind is dominant, and safety is paramount.

When I was in kindergarten, another young girl invited me to come to lunch at her house. This was an entirely new experience for me, and after getting my mother's approval, the plans were put in place.

The school was situated halfway between my friend's house and mine. I walked to school every day, following a path behind my house through large open fields, while she walked to school every day through her neighborhood.

My friend was from a Swedish family, which meant nothing to me at five years old. All I knew was that I liked her. When we arrived at her house and walked inside, everything changed in an instant. There was nothing in her house that was familiar to me. Their furniture was different from ours, and their house was arranged in a way I didn't recognize.

Worst of all, their food was different. I believe her mother was cooking a special Swedish lunch for us, and from the moment I stepped in the door and smelled those foreign smells and realized everything was different, my five-year-old mind started to melt down. I was horribly frightened and didn't know why, and started crying uncontrollably.

My friend's mother was a gentle and kind woman. She tried to comfort me, but I was beyond consolation and only wanted to return home. After a few minutes, I was granted permission to leave, and I ran all the way home, crying the whole way.

As I look back on that scene now, I ache to hold my five-year-old self and let her cry out her fear. She was acting instinctively to the threat of the unknown and had no idea why it frightened her so badly. At five, she had no rational thinking abilities to rely on and was completely unprepared to embrace the new and different.

If I could, I would also go back and thank that mother for her kindness and apologize for being so inconsolable. I'm sure it was a distressing experience for her and my friend, too.

Fortunately, as you grow up and are introduced to new people, situations, and environments, you learn to incorporate them into what is familiar to you. Your world gradually widens to include many new people and situations that would frighten you at a younger age.

However, even in adulthood, it is never wise to underestimate the power of the familiar in your day-to-day life, either personally or professionally. Every time you step into the unknown, that instinctive fear is there to greet you.

Adam's Story

Take, for example, my client, whom I'll call Adam, who ignored his fear of the unknown for so long that it began to show up as a physical disability.

Another client referred Adam to me because he was experiencing a lack of balance that medicine couldn't resolve. Adam's access to the medical community was wide and deep, and he'd been to every type of doctor imaginable. He'd undergone extensive testing through multiple large institutions, and they could find nothing physically wrong with him.

Adam's lack of balance was interesting because it only occurred when he tried to move forward. He was fine while seated, but the instant he tried to walk forward, he felt out of balance. Interestingly, his lack of balance was not visible in his gait or posture; it was only discernible to him, and he felt it constantly. He suffered from this lack of balance for years. It was never bad enough that he couldn't move at all; it simply meant that every forward step he took was uncomfortable.

As Adam and I discussed what might be causing this lack of balance, we considered the extreme stress he was under at work, where he had a lot of responsibility, and in his marriage, which had devolved into duty. He told me he felt "indifferent" about his marriage, even though he'd been married for decades and had grown children.

Adam had once been very good at sports and remembered being able to walk across an elevated board with ease. His present lack of balance annoyed and frightened him because it was a problem he couldn't solve.

Together, we took several steps to investigate the root cause of Adam's balance issues. We healed some past trauma and explored why he felt disconnected from his true self. Adam was a deeply spiritual person who valued the sanctity of marriage. He vigorously resisted admitting to himself that his marriage might be slowly debilitating him and completely rejected the possibility of separation or divorce.

Finally, we decided to talk to the part of Adam that was feeling out of balance directly in hypnosis because that part held all the answers. Although this may seem strange to those who have never worked in hypnosis, it is a very common technique used to navigate conflict between competing needs and values.

This was Adam's breakthrough. Maintaining his spiritual life was one of his highest values, and he could clearly identify that he was hampering his spiritual wellness to protect a marriage that was no longer spiritually alive. This allowed him to make a clear decision about what he needed to move forward into the unknown without conflict.

Adam's fear of the unknown, specifically separation or divorce, was heightened by his spiritual conflict, which told him those possibilities were wrong. It was only when he could resolve the spiritual conflict that he could take the risk of stepping into the unknown. Many internal struggles are like this. There is a basic underlying fear and then a values issue that exacerbates it.

When you can identify the underlying fear, you are halfway to solving the problem, and the subconscious fear of the unknown is always a good place to start.

Whether you are stepping into the unknown by giving a presentation at work, taking on a new project, dating a new person, learning a new skill, moving to a new city, or even doing something as mundane as experimenting with a new diet, it is wise to remember your subconscious mind's bias toward the familiar. Once you see and acknowledge it, you can make a rational decision about what is truly dangerous and what is not.

Your subconscious mind is always on your side, working hard to protect you and keep you safe. Once it is informed and aligned with your goals and desires, it will look for ways to help you achieve them. At that point, your most powerful ally is working for you instead of against you, and you become unstoppable.

GEMS

- The subconscious mind equates familiarity with safety, causing everything unknown to become automatically dangerous.

- It is most helpful to stop and question why you are feeling fear so you can determine if this is simply something unknown and, therefore, frightening to the subconscious mind or a real threat that you need to pay attention to.

- Your subconscious mind can be your most powerful ally or your worst enemy, depending on how you communicate with it.

Chapter 15

Making Change Easier

Creating peace of mind always involves big change. Every human on the planet endures problems and emotional wounds as they make their way through life, and these need to be addressed and resolved so you can allow peace to grow. Remember, "No one skates." No one glides through life effortlessly without picking up habits, wounds, beliefs, and fears that prevent them from living their dreams.

When it comes to big change, you have a choice of how to accomplish it. You can initiate change through your conscious mind or your subconscious mind, but your experience will be radically different depending on what you choose.

- When you change from the conscious mind, you gather knowledge and understanding and exert willpower.
- When you change from the subconscious mind, you allow the subconscious mind to shift and notice the results.
- When you change from the conscious mind, you change despite fears or toxic beliefs and force your way forward no matter what.
- When you change from the subconscious mind, you resolve and/or heal fears and toxic beliefs and watch as the subconscious mind sends you different emotional signals.
- When you change from the conscious mind, it feels hard.
- When you change from the subconscious mind, it feels surprisingly easy. You begin to feel like you've always been this new way because it feels so natural.

As you begin your journey of change, some of the steps are the same, regardless of which approach you choose.

The first step is to decide to change. That decision might arise out of an unwillingness to live with emotional, psychological, or spiritual pain anymore, or it might be inspired by a desire to improve at something or to accomplish a specific goal. Regardless of the motivation, the first step is to clearly decide to change.

Second, you must decide how you will create the change you want. What do you need? Does this change require guidance and support, and if so, what kind of guidance and support do you need? Many people go wrong at this juncture and shame themselves into believing that they can create the change they so fervently desire completely on their own.

Whether you choose guidance or not, support is always necessary when embarking on a big change, and it is wise to have that support in place first. That could be friends, family, mentors, or professional support.

Third, you must commit to the change you want. You must be 100 percent sure that this change is what you want and know that you will do whatever it takes to create it.

At this point, you are ready.

My client, whom I will call Jeremy, was in this state of readiness when he first came to see me.

Jeremy's Story

Jeremy's passion in life was music. He played multiple instruments, some of which he built himself. When he wasn't playing music, he was listening to it or thinking about it. He loved all genres of music and participated in several local orchestras as well as a jazz band.

He was feeling frustrated and defeated when he came to see me because he would freeze up whenever he played in public. Solos were a particular agony, as his hands shook, and he could not finger notes correctly. He got confused and would lose his place in the music.

He told me that he had experienced this problem throughout his life, but lately, it was much worse. Interestingly, it never happened when he was practicing, either alone or with other people. He loved sharing his music and played well in the company of other musicians if it wasn't in public.

"What do you want?" I asked him.

"I want to enjoy my music," he said. The importance of this clearly articulated desire cannot be overstated. Jeremy didn't want to be a virtuoso, a famous musician, or even the best player in the city. He did not lust after status or acclaim. He wanted to feel happy and in flow when he played in front of an audience. He wanted to experience the exalted state of being in complete sync with the other musicians.

We started our work together by writing down his self-talk. What was he telling himself, I asked, as he was playing in public? It was a frightening list. "My tone sucks. I'm playing the rhythm wrong. People know I'm not confident. My presentation is amateurish. I'm messing up. Everyone sees how nervous I am. I should have practiced more," were some of the belittling thoughts he chanted to himself every time he played before an audience.

With thoughts like that, it's amazing he could play at all. It was easy to understand why he felt tortured.

I wondered aloud where this inner judgmental voice came from. Jeremy had no doubt that it came from his father, who demeaned and criticized him throughout his life. Jeremy's father tyrannized everyone around him. No one was good enough to please his father, but Jeremy, as the oldest son, took the brunt of his poisonous abuse.

Over time, his father's constant criticism seeped into his psyche until Jeremy began to persecute himself with the same toxic messages. After decades of repeatedly thinking those thoughts, they turned into pernicious beliefs deeply rooted in his subconscious mind.

It was time for Jeremy to reclaim his power and disarm the tyrant within. During hypnosis, Jeremy imagined a place where he was safe and protected. He then invited his father to meet him in his inner safe and protected place and informed him that the purpose of the visit was for his father to return the power he had stolen from Jeremy.

His father complained and criticized him, but Jeremy wouldn't back down. His father eventually complied, and when Jeremy had his power back, he thanked his father for coming and told him to leave.

On the surface, this sounds like a strange procedure, one that the conscious mind would reject without a second thought. However, the subconscious does not understand the difference between a vividly imagined event and a real event, so in Jeremy's subconscious mind, this event actually took place. The tyrant was neutralized, and Jeremy now owned his power.

The impact was life-altering, all because the subconscious mind understood the significance of this one imagined event.

Jeremy could release his need to constantly criticize himself and view his playing with fresh eyes. At that point, we could take direct aim at the self-talk.

Creating Freedom

We began by writing statements that were the exact opposite of what he told himself. Some of his new self-talk was: "When I play music in public, my tone is beautiful and steady. When I play music in public, my rhythm is just right. When I play music in public, people sense my confidence. When I play music in public, my presentation is professional. I practice exactly the right amount. When I play music in public, my hands are steady and sure."

In hypnosis, we repeated these new self-statements to his subconscious mind and backed it up with detailed visualizations of him playing beautifully in public, feeling completely comfortable and relaxed. He saw himself as not caring if he made a mistake here and there and only being interested in creating great music that the musicians and audience loved. When he gave his subconscious mind a clear image of that, with all his joyful feelings connected to it, the subconscious mind knew Jeremy was no longer in danger and changed the signals it sent to him.

Over a period of three sessions, Jeremy stopped sabotaging himself with toxic thoughts and stepped into his passion with freedom and joy he had never felt before. As a bonus, his technical skills improved, too.

Jeremy's subconscious mind had been operating under an old belief that every nasty thing his father said to him was true, that he was a terrible musician, that he always made mistakes, and that everyone could tell he was an amateur. Once those old beliefs were neutralized and new beliefs were embraced, his subconscious mind sent Jeremy signals of fun and enjoyment when he played music in public instead of fear and despair.

Repeated criticism from a young age is a toxic wound that relentlessly leaks poison into your mind. The wound can then fester beneath the surface for decades, leaving you frightened, depressed, and insecure even when you know you have the talent and drive to succeed.

In Jeremy's case, the criticism was so bad that he felt powerless to change. Everything changed once his subconscious mind saw Jeremy take back his power, heard the new statements he was making about himself, and experienced his joy at playing in public through his visualizations.

Jeremy had tried many times to overcome his fear of playing in public in the past. Only when the subconscious mind was aligned with that change could his love and infectious enthusiasm for music shine through.

Changing from the subconscious mind is surprisingly fast and easy because your subconscious mind wants to help you. All it needs is up-to-date information.

When Jeremy walked out of my office for the last time, it was as if he had always believed in himself. Playing beautifully in public was just the way he was now. He was finally free to enjoy his music.

GEMS

Pause and reflect on these essential ideas.

- To change, you must first make a firm decision to change. The second step is to decide how you will accomplish the change, and the third is to commit to the change.

- Change is easier when you allow the subconscious mind to take the lead.

- Your subconscious mind wants to help you. All it needs is updated information.

Part Three

Peace of Mind

- Developing peace of mind intentionally is easier with reliable tools, such as observing your life from a detached point of view or directly dealing with a troubling emotion.
- Peace of mind is a cultivated state that requires an ongoing commitment and desire to live in peace.
- Maintaining peace of mind means you are willing to resolve and let go of every emotion, belief, or thought that doesn't serve your highest good. Why would you keep them?

Chapter 16

How to Have Peace of Mind

The one thing clients request most in my practice is peace of mind, and oh, how I would love to hand that to them on a platter.

The problem is that I cannot "give" peace of mind to my clients. First, they must heal the wounds, preventing them from feeling it. Second, they must consciously invite peace of mind into their lives. Those two steps are the main framework of *The Peace of Mind Blueprint*.

However, before we fill in all the Blueprint details, let's pause for a moment and define peace of mind: what it is, what it's not, and what it could be.

The *Merriam-Webster Dictionary* defines peace of mind as "a feeling of being safe or protected." This is an astute observation, as safety is a primal need. Fear, the emotion that haunts so many in forms ranging from anxiety to terror, is the feeling of a lack of safety, and fear can trigger multiple forms of suffering and behavioral problems.

I like this definition up to a point. Indeed, a sense of safety is essential to peace of mind, but it is also possible to feel safe and not have peace of mind. For instance, I can feel safe in my home and family and still be angry, upset, irritated, or worried, and that's not very peaceful.

Vocabulary.com describes peace of mind as "a state in which your brain is calm, at ease, and untroubled by worry." This is an excellent addition to the definition if you change the word "brain" to "mind" because brain and mind are different. The brain is a physical organ that can be dead or alive. It's possible to inspect the brain of a person who has died, for instance, but it is impossible to visually inspect a mind in any circumstance.

Despite remarkable strides in brain research, the mind, be it conscious or subconscious, remains invisible to the human eye. Even with MRI scans, scientists cannot pinpoint a specific location in the brain and declare, "This is your mind." Neuroscientist Heather Berlin suggests that the mind is best understood as a dynamic process of neural connections, not a tangible entity.

Combining the two previous definitions, we can describe peace of mind as a state in which one feels safe and protected and one's mind is calm, at ease, and untroubled by worry.

I like this definition, but for me, at least, it is incomplete.

According to Wikipedia, peace of mind "may refer to inner peace, a deliberate state of psychological or spiritual calm despite the potential presence of stressors."

Here, we find the missing piece: "a deliberate state." Peace of mind is not floating in the air waiting to be captured, nor is it a temporary state of mind that comes and goes of its own volition. Peace of mind is the result of deliberate effort and practice.

Combining the three descriptions, we arrive at this definition:

Peace of mind is a deliberate and cultivated state in which one feels safe, calm, relaxed, and free from worry despite potential stressors.

This is an empowering definition because it puts peace of mind in your control. You have the power to create and sustain peace of mind by choice and practice. This is excellent news. Peace of mind is not something you have to chase. It is yours to develop if you choose to.

So, the components of peace of mind are:

- Intentionally chosen and practiced
- Safety and protection
- Calm and tranquility
- Being fully present, regardless of circumstances

Where's the Owner's Manual?

Much of this book has been devoted to explaining how to heal traumas, negative emotions, and toxic beliefs trapped in the subconscious mind that trigger suffering in the present.

This is where most people start their journey, and it is, unfortunately, sometimes where they stop. They come for hypnotherapy because of emotional pain they can't resolve. When the pain stops, they leave believing that peace of mind will naturally develop.

It is important to understand that although healing the wounds in the subconscious mind is an essential first step, it does not complete the transformation process. Creating peace of mind requires sustained practice and effort to adopt new mental and emotional habits and the ability to visualize and embrace a future once thought to be impossible.

The rewards are worth it. Imagine being able to stay calm in any circumstance. Imagine being emotionally unreactive when another person is angry, abusive, or disrespectful. You suddenly become immune to manipulation because you can choose how to respond based on rational thought and compassionate intent instead of being baited into a reaction you might later regret.

This does not mean you bury and ignore your feelings. It means you can process them peacefully and productively, leading to resolution instead of breakdown. It means you recognize what you are feeling but call on a deep well of peace, self-trust, safety, and stability within your mind to navigate whatever situation you encounter.

It means you value your peace of mind so much that you won't waste your time and energy being emotionally reactive.

Does this sound impossible? Does this sound like a talent only the most spiritual can develop? I can almost hear you thinking, *I'm not trying to be the Buddha, Sherris. I'm just trying to get through life the best I can.*

What if I told you this is your birthright? What if I told you that developing this ability makes not only your life unimaginably better, easier, and more pleasant but the lives of every person you encounter as well?

Humans are born with the most incredible powers and abilities on earth, but no one shows us how to use them. Where is the owner's manual? Where are the instructions? Why aren't we teaching kindergarteners to calm their nervous system with their breathing, create love and compassion for themselves and others, and develop peace in their minds? These are skills they will use their whole lives. These are life's essential skills, but we are left to discover them for ourselves.

The Blueprint

You will recognize some of the steps to peace of mind from previous chapters, while others will be new.

Most importantly, remember that developing peace of mind means you are willing to give up every emotion, belief, or thought that doesn't serve your highest good. Why would you keep them?

This requires lifelong dedication, consistent introspection, and an ability to ask at any juncture, "Does this emotion, belief, or thought serve me right now? Does feeling this emotion, believing this belief, or thinking this thought make me feel good, happy, content, or peaceful? If it doesn't, what do I choose instead?"

Sometimes, this task is more accessible than others, depending on how triggered you are in the present moment. I am the first to state that I stumble and fall frequently as I walk this path. And that's okay. It's all just practice.

Imagine a figure skater practicing their routine, a basketball player practicing their shots, or a diver practicing their dives. They will all stumble and fall now and then, but the more they practice, the stronger and more skilled they become and the greater ease they experience. It's the same when you train your mind.

Everything Can Be Easier

Practice is repetition, and repetition is one of the primary languages of the subconscious mind. Through consistent, dedicated practice, you communicate to your subconscious mind what you want. If you support that practice with joyful feelings, you communicate in two of the subconscious mind's primary languages. And if you visualize the result of your practice positively, you are speaking three of the languages of the subconscious mind. Imagine the impact that will have on your life. You are now collaborating with the most significant, most powerful part of your mind, and you haven't even gone into a trance.

The Blueprint

So, without further introduction, here are the steps to developing peace of mind.

1. Want peace of mind with every fiber of your being.
2. Commit to the process. Know you'll succeed.
3. Identify and acknowledge what's holding you back.
4. Heal any trauma or persistent negative emotions.
   a. Choose the positive emotions you wish to feel instead.
   b. Practice moving into the new state.
5. Identify and dissolve toxic or debilitating beliefs.
   a. Choose new, empowering beliefs.
   b. Support and reinforce those new beliefs.
6. Practice consistent introspection
   a. Adopt a willingness to change.

Now, here's a statement that should be printed in big, bold letters in *The Owner's Manual For Human Beings*:

Every step of this process is faster and easier when you use psycho-spiritual hypnosis to communicate with the subconscious mind. Every. Single. Step.

The above list can seem overwhelming or even impossible to the conscious mind. However, to the subconscious mind, every step on that list is simply an inner shift. All it needs is guidance and new information.

Once the subconscious mind makes that shift, you feel better and have more energy, your creativity blossoms, and you move forward with growing enthusiasm.

How Much Fun Is That?

To quote British hypnotherapist Freddy Jacquin, "How much fun is that?" How much fun is it to purposely create the life you want? How much fun is it to succeed at goals you once thought impossible? How much fun is it to choose how you want to feel? How much fun is it to be creative, enthusiastic, and energized? I can tell you from experience it's pretty darn fun.

Peace of mind develops as you move through each step. It is a gradual and cumulative process that builds over time. You feel remarkably better and create a sense of inner spaciousness each time you heal an emotional wound or deactivate a toxic belief.

You plant the positive emotions, thoughts, and beliefs you want to adopt into the spaciousness you create by releasing those negative influences. Then, you nurture those emotions, thoughts, and beliefs with love, attention, and persistence.

The more specific you are in educating the subconscious mind about what you want, and the more dedicated you are to maintaining the new state you desire with practice, the farther you go and the faster you change.

So, ask yourself: "How far do I want to go? What am I willing to do to get there?"

GEMS

Pause and reflect on these essential ideas.

- Peace of mind is a deliberately cultivated state in which one feels secure, calm, relaxed, and free from worry despite potential stressors.
- Through consistent, dedicated practice, you communicate to your subconscious mind what you want.
- The six steps to peace of mind are:
    1. Want peace of mind with every fiber of your being.
    2. Commit to the process. Know you'll succeed.
    3. Identify and acknowledge what's holding you back.
    4. Heal any trauma or persistent negative emotions.
    5. Identify and dissolve toxic or debilitating beliefs.
    6. Practice consistent introspection.
- Peace of mind develops as you move through each step. It is a gradual and cumulative process that builds over time.

Chapter 17

The Power of Witnessing

The greatest thief of peace of mind is emotional reactivity.

People often become emotionally reactive when circumstances or events trigger a reaction caused by past wounds. As you can see from the examples in my life, as well as Emily's, Mary's, Adam's, and Jeremy's experiences, old wounds affect our behavior in the present, even when we are unaware of it.

People also become emotionally reactive when they feel violated or out of control. The emotional reactivity can range from rage to weeping because whatever has happened has triggered the sympathetic nervous system and ignited the fight-flight-freeze response.

One of your greatest allies in preventing the theft of your peace of mind by emotional reactivity is the ability to witness. You have an inner witness, just as you have an inner critic. While the inner critic constantly tells you everything you're doing wrong, the inner witness notices what's happening without judgment. The inner witness provides practical information you can use to make wise decisions *if* you are willing to listen.

Let's look at a simple example. You step on the scale and see the number has gone up. Your inner critic immediately jumps in, saying something like, "You're so fat! You're disgusting! How could you let yourself get this way? Now, you'll never be thin again." Your inner witness looks at the scale and says, "You've gained twenty pounds."

The inner critic shames you loudly. The inner witness states information without judgment. *The inner critic prevents you from changing by assuming your failure in advance. The inner witness assumes nothing, leaving the choice up to you.*

It's important to remember that the inner critic's voice is loud and relentless, while the witness's voice is soft, sometimes only a whisper. You must intentionally pay attention to the witness's voice again and again.

Witnessing Anger

Anger is one of those emotions that can make almost anyone emotionally reactive. People say and do things in anger that they would likely never say and do if they were calm and in control because, left to run amuck, anger is like a forest fire destroying everything in its path.

It doesn't have to be that way when you understand that *anger is our most primitive way of setting boundaries.* When you get angry, you are backing something off, saying no, and refusing to let something into your world. It would, of course, be emotionally less taxing to set a boundary without anger, but when your back is against a wall and you've run out of options, anger will come to your aid.

For many years, I experienced my own puzzle with anger. As a rule, I am not usually an angry person, yet there were times when I would experience a fiery burst of anger that always took me by surprise and left me exhausted from the sudden flood of adrenaline and cortisol coursing through my body.

It would take days for all the stress chemicals to drain away, and I could easily spiral down into a low-level depression as

I tried to cope with the situation. I hated every second of the experience.

After some time, I made the decision to activate my witness and monitor my behavior when I felt angry. Since I didn't get angry frequently, this process took a couple of years and required a lot of patience. The results, however, were life changing. I gained a clear understanding of what triggered my anger and learned how to intervene early to resolve the situation before my body was flooded with stress chemicals, making it difficult for me to think clearly.

The process was simple. Any time I felt anger, I immediately stopped what I was doing and asked myself, "What is happening *right now*? What *exactly* am I reacting to?" This step took time and patience at first, but when I sifted through everything that had happened within an hour before I felt angry, I could point to the moment the anger erupted and know that was the trigger.

Once I had the trigger, I would ponder it and determine why I was angry. On one occasion, I was reacting to someone lying to me. On another, I was reacting to someone acting with a lack of integrity and not living up to what they had promised. The next time, I was reacting to someone standing too close to me, causing me to feel physically trapped.

Over the course of about two years, I came to understand that I got angry every time someone violated one of my core values or my personal space. It was so simple.

Now, the minute I feel anger, I simply look for the violation and take appropriate action before the anger develops its engine and runs wild in my mind.

For me to activate my witness and use the information productively, I had to:

1. Notice immediately any time I felt anger.
2. Stop whatever I was doing and look closely at what was happening right that minute.
3. Identify the trigger.
4. Determine why I was angry.
5. Categorize the trigger (what sort of violation was it).
6. Decide what action to take to resolve the situation.

I have practiced this process so many times now that it happens almost instantly, and I no longer labor over the individual steps. I move from anger to resolution in minutes rather than days or weeks. This has saved me a tremendous amount of time and energy that I can now use for positive purposes rather than emotional recovery.

This is the power of the witness. It gives you actionable information you can use to better navigate your life.

Witnessing Supports Every Step of *The Peace Of Mind Blueprint.*

The witness is the part of us that lives in a state of detached observation, simply noticing what's happening without judgment or interpretation. When you access that information with curiosity and good intent, you are empowered to make the best possible decision for you in every circumstance.

Step One of the Blueprint is to want peace of mind with every fiber of your being. Well, how do you even know that you want peace of mind? To get to this first step, you engage your witness to notice you don't have it. You look at the conditions of your life from a detached state of mind and realize that however you are living, whether that is chaos, confusion, powerlessness, depression, despair, or some other negative state, you clearly do not have peace of mind.

Then, you open yourself to the possibility that peace of mind is possible and available to you and want that with the full force of your being.

Step Two of the Blueprint is to commit to peace of mind and know you will succeed. Committing to creating peace of mind in your life means calling on your witness to consider your options with detached curiosity, weighing the pros and cons of each, and deciding which path will best serve your needs.

Knowing you'll succeed requires the detached perspective of the witness. You must look at your life conditions without emotion or judgment, decide you are no longer willing to tolerate those conditions, and know that nothing other than peace of mind will satisfy you.

Step Three of *The Peace Of Mind Blueprint* is to identify and acknowledge what's holding you back. This step is almost impossible without the detached point of view of the witness because when you move into your witness, it's like taking a big step back to look at the whole of your life and dispassionately identifying the obstacles in your way.

People often want to deny the obstacles in front of them, to wish them away, and pretend they aren't there. This won't get you very far. Clearly identifying the obstacles in your path is the pivotal step to taking appropriate action.

If this step is difficult for you, I can help you with that. Sometimes, you need an objective view to pinpoint the obstacles you face. They may have become so familiar that they are invisible to you.

Step Four is to heal any traumas or persistent negative emotions preventing you from moving forward. Once your inner landscape's "big rocks" have been identified (step three), the value of working in a guided hypnotic trance becomes clear.

When you are hypnotized, you easily see things from that coveted detached point of view of the witness. You can also observe the larger patterns at work without day-to-day emotional reactivity interfering. This makes decisions faster and easier, and you send your subconscious mind the very clear message that you are ready to heal.

Step Five is to identify and dissolve any toxic or debilitating beliefs. Like steps three and four, this can be challenging without guidance. Beliefs that are toxic and debilitating are often picked up in early childhood when your conscious mind is not yet active. They may be so deeply ingrained that they feel natural. You may not even know you have them.

Dissolving these beliefs may be a matter of seeing them from a different perspective or healing a past event that set them in place. Both processes are easier to accomplish with help.

Step Six is to practice consistent introspection and adopt a willingness to change. At this point in the process, you have relaxed and are committed to keeping peace of mind. You have chosen the positive thoughts and emotions you want to plant in your subconscious mind and are practicing nurturing them. You are familiar with significant change and looking at your life from the point of view of the witness.

It becomes clear that change is always happening, and detached introspection allows you to keep track of it so events or circumstances you did not expect do not derail you.

Change Is Practice

Most of us grew up believing that change happens to us and that we are the passive receivers of change. After all, our bodies grow and mature seemingly of their own accord. The culture around us changes due to visible—and invisible—forces out of our control. The very planet we live on shakes and erupts in terrifying change regardless of its effect on us as individuals.

However, the most important change you ever experience is in your mind, which is entirely within your control. Intentional growth is both possible and necessary for all humans. You came into this world with powerful abilities, and now you put them to good use for your highest good. And as a wonderful bonus, as you heal and grow yourself, you take part in healing and growing humanity.

Awareness is the first step in that process, and the witness is the part of us that brings that awareness to our attention in a useful and actionable form.

As you practice listening to the witness, you gain a new best friend. A friend who is there for you every second of your life. A friend who supports you with steady consistency. The witness needs only to be listened to, and you are automatically on the path of change.

Practice. Practice listening, pondering, and observing what is really happening in your life. Start with awareness, intentionally listen to the witness, and take control of your life.

What have you got to lose?

GEMS

Pause and reflect on these essential ideas.

- The greatest thief of peace of mind is emotional reactivity, and one of our greatest allies in preventing the theft of our peace of mind through emotional reactivity is the ability to witness.
- The inner witness simply notices what's happening without judgment and provides us with practical information we can use to make wise decisions.
- Anger is our most primitive means of setting a boundary, and we can identify the triggers and preempt emotional reactivity before it starts.
- Witnessing supports every step of *The Peace Of Mind Blueprint*.
- The witness needs only to be listened to, and you are automatically on the path of change.

Chapter 18

Emotional Messengers and Keeping Peace of Mind

As you heal old wounds and plant the positive thoughts and emotions that you want to develop in your subconscious mind, you create space for peace of mind to take root.

Nourishing and supporting your new thoughts and emotions empowers your peace of mind to grow, gather strength, and begin to bloom. You become more discerning about the sorts of relationships you want to invite into your life. You become more decisive and confident about which activities you choose to engage in.

You grow disinterested in conflict and drama and begin to understand that there is a whole world of beauty and kindness beyond the chaos. You couldn't see the world of beauty and kindness before. However, now you can, and nothing else will satisfy you. You find that grounded equanimity that allows you to make decisions with a clear mind and an open heart.

However, having peace of mind doesn't mean that life stops happening. Peace of mind is not a fairy-tale happiness ever after. New events and circumstances are constantly cycling through your daily experience and arousing emotions of all kinds. The difference is that having invested in healing your wounds and developing peace of mind, these events and circumstances can be navigated with more ease.

Confusing Sadness

For example, I often experienced a sadness that would come and go for reasons I could not decipher. When It came over me again recently, I asked myself, "Why now?"

Is this just a habit? I wondered.

Is it my brain's way of holding on to the status quo, maintaining what has always been?

Is it a tactic to keep me from moving forward?

Is it my comfort zone because I have felt it for so long that I can't imagine my life without it?

None of these possibilities felt right.

As I look back on my life, I see profound loss and searing grief, but this feeling of sadness was not that, and I had been confusing them.

This feeling of sadness was like an ache that started in the center of my abdomen and radiated out until it saturated every muscle and fiber of my being. There was no part of me that did not hurt.

In the past, I had tried ignoring it and befriending it. I had wondered why it was there and given up in frustration. I had accepted it and rejected it. I had argued with the sadness, but mostly, I just wished it would go away.

What I never did was ask the sadness directly why it was there. So, using self-hypnosis, I asked this sadness, "Why are you here?"

It's hard to describe this process and what it feels like. You ask a part of yourself a question and wait for the answer. The answer comes as a thought in your mind. It's like having ESP with a single part of yourself.

When I asked the question, I thought about being broken. I didn't know what that meant, so I kept asking questions until the thought, "You're separated from yourself," was in my mind. Then, I understood. Earlier that day, I had been in an environment that left me feeling emotionally numb. Shortly thereafter, the aching sadness started.

The sadness I was experiencing was a numbness buster. It was letting me know that I had spaced out, gone away, exited stage left. I had stopped being present because the environment was painful. The sadness was letting me know that I needed to take care of myself in a safer environment so I could feel whole again.

Coming out of hypnosis, I felt relieved. Now that I understood the message, I could spend my energy solving the problem instead of trying to kill the messenger.

The messages I receive from emotion are likely not the messages that you will receive. You are an individual, expressing yourself in your own way. However, the mechanism for discovering the message is the same for you as it is for me. Your emotions are messengers. Receiving the message is what's important.

In hypnotherapy, communicating with one specific aspect of yourself is called parts work. Many of my clients have had big aha moments during this process that are paradoxically both surprising and obvious.

Experiencing this process again increased my respect for its simple power. What a gift to understand what this aching sadness was telling me. Yes, I was feeling a loss, but it was the loss of my own presence, and that I can fix.

Now, when I feel it, I say, "Thank you for letting me know I am feeling separated from myself. I will take care of that." Emotions are always messengers. When their message seems uncertain, the direct approach is often the best approach to getting answers.

Sadness has been a constant visitor in my life, one that I used to get caught in for long periods of time. Now that I understand this more recent variation, I don't have to get caught there. I can hear its message and take action to reconnect with myself by delving into something I love, like talking with a trusted friend or going for a walk in the woods—in short, being me again. These are simple solutions for a feeling that used to haunt me endlessly.

Your peace of mind doesn't evaporate if you stumble, or your environment suddenly becomes chaotic. You know that you can access that calm, tranquil sanctuary deep inside again because now you know what it feels like, and that feeling guides you back to equanimity.

A while back, I wrote a poem about finding my way back to peace of mind that I offer here for your inspiration and enjoyment. It's called "I Remember."

I Remember

When my heart is broken
And my soul aches from loss,
When a voice deep inside
Moans in pain,
When even my body collapses
Under the weight of broken dreams,
I remember.
I remember that
I have done this before.
I remember drowning
In relentless waves
Of grief and despair
That should have killed me
But didn't.

And I wonder
Is this the time
that I dissolve
and disappear?

Is this the time
My lungs stop breathing
My heart stops beating
My soul takes flight?

But then,
When I have almost given up hope
My wounded heart heals,
My body strengthens,
My soul shines again,
And I am granted
One more moment of grace.
One more chance
To embody
The awe and wonder
Of living again.
One more chance
To love again,
One more chance
To laugh again,
One more chance
To thrive in joy
again.

May you embody the awe and wonder of living again, loving again, and thriving in joy again.

May you rediscover the joy of being your most essential self with peace in your mind, love in your heart, and joy in your spirit.

GEMS

Pause and reflect on these essential ideas.

- Having peace of mind doesn't mean that life stops happening; there are always new things to respond to.
- Your peace of mind doesn't evaporate if you stumble. Deep inside, there is still a well of peace and tranquility to draw from.
- Emotions are messengers letting you know there is something you need to pay attention to.
- Ask an emotion why it is there and relax enough to receive the answer.
- You can embody the awe and wonder of living again, loving again, and thriving in joy again.
- You can rediscover the joy of being your most essential self with peace in your mind, love in your heart, and joy in your spirit.

I would love to hear from you!

Reach out to me at **ThePeaceOfMindBlueprint.com.**

Send me your biggest Ah Ha's!
Let me know what resonated with you the most.
Set up an appointment to chat.
My door is open.

Sherri's

Wrapping Up

Beautiful reader,

Thank you for embarking on this journey with me. Let's review what you've learned:

- Understanding how your mind works and how you can use psycho-spiritual hypnosis to heal your emotional and spiritual wounds, enabling you to create a life filled with peace and joy.
- Recognizing that most therapeutic protocols for emotional and spiritual healing focus on the conscious mind, while the obstacles to your wellness are in your subconscious mind.
- Realizing that psycho-spiritual hypnosis excels in communicating directly with your subconscious mind, where

you can heal the core wounds holding you back and foster natural change and evolution.

- Acknowledging that your subconscious mind constitutes ninety percent of your mind, and without access to it, your ability to heal and resolve underlying issues is severely limited.

- Gaining a comprehensive understanding of psycho-spiritual hypnosis, its benefits, and the various problems it can address.

- Discovering how your subconscious mind can become your most valuable ally instead of your worst enemy.

- Examining real-life examples of my healing journey and that of some of my clients, illustrating the profound transformations achievable through psycho-spiritual hypnosis.

- Defining peace of mind—clarifying what it is and what it isn't and providing insight into the experience of living with a foundation of well-being that nurtures continued balance and harmony.

If you desire a better life, a deeper understanding of the messages your emotions are sending you, and ease in navigating life's circumstances, I urge you to schedule a thirty-minute chat with me. In thirty minutes, we can discover if psycho-spiritual hypnosis is a good healing modality for you and what you can accomplish with it.

* I would love to hear from you! Reach out to me at ThePeaceOfMindBlueprint.com.
* Send me your biggest Ah Ha's! Let me know what resonated with you the most. Set up an appointment to chat. My door is open. Sherris

Acknowledgments

To my clients, this book stands as a testament to the trust and faith you place in me and all that I have learned from you. You inspire me every day. Thank you, I am profoundly grateful.

To Cheryl Beshada and Frank Garfield, my teachers at the Clinical Hypnosis Institute, thank you for introducing me to the world of hypnosis, for presenting the massive amount of information with clarity and precision, and for the endless patience and goodwill you showed in the process. It all began with you.

To Ben Gioia, my exceptional book-writing coach, thank you for your patience, guidance, deep knowledge, and encouragement. Without you, this book might have died inside me, and I would mourn that loss.

To all my other hypnotherapy teachers—Lori Hammond, Melissa Tiers, Freddy Jacquin, Nicholas Spohn, Barry Neale, and Katherine Zimmerman—I learn and grow from everything you have taught me.

To Kev Webster, thank you for writing the insightful foreword for this book and your tireless support. I am honored by your perceptions, enthusiasm, and friendship.

To Lena Rush, who created the cover art and wonderful illustrations for this book: Thank you. Your art makes this a better, more accessible book.

To my family and friends, who listened to me talk about this book with interest and patience. Thank you for your unwavering love and support.

To you, my readers, for your curiosity and openness to new ideas and new ways of healing, my profound thank you. I can't wait to hear from you.

www.ingramcontent.com/pod-product-compliance
Lightning Source LLC
Chambersburg PA
CBHW020307010526
44107CB00001B/13